YOUR UNCONDITIONED

Inner Magic

BY KITTY O'BRIEN

Promotional Page

CONTENTS

Acknowledgements

I want to thank:

Martin O'Brien, my amazing Uncle, for editing the book for me, and helping me to strengthen my writing.

Justyna Matejek and Kelly Rothery for their knowledge of the mind.

Natalie Tiley-Walker, thank you, thank you, thank you. You were my rock through it all and still are. You are my Soul Sister, and I love you dearly.

Michaela Chapman, thank you for your unwavering faith in me, and supporting me during my abuse, leaving my abusive partner and afterwards, and coaching me through the Court System.

Jax Emilio Robinson, my mentor and inspiration.

Vickie J Parris, my soul sister and inspiration.

A special thank you to all my family and friends who never stopped believing in me.

From the deepest part of my heart, a very special thank you to my son Harrison, who gave me wisdom, courage and strength. Harrison, you sparked that maternal instinct to act and broke the chains that kept me from flying. With your help, we soar high amongst the clouds. Harrison, you are my Stardust, and I love you more than words can describe.

Dedication

For anyone who has hit rock bottom, feels "stuck", tired of their current situation, who knows there is more to their life than "this", for anyone who dares to dream.

"All men dream; but not equally. Those who dream by night in the dusty recesses of their minds Awake to find that it was vanity; But the dreamers of day are dangerous men. That they may act their dreams with open eyes to make it possible."

T. E. Lawrence (1888 – 1935)

British Archaeologist, Army Officer, Diplomat, and Writer

Life is a roller coaster, and I have experienced many highs and lows. First, I lost everything, and with the help of loving family, friends and mentors, I found all I would ever need.

Thank you.

Thank you for your unconditional love, guidance, inspiration, and belief in me.

Preface

We all have a higher purpose, and we must change our mindset to find this. Through society and years of programming, also known as conditioning, we have lost the ability to dream. As a result, we live in scarcity, not abundance. We can have anything the heart desires by changing our belief systems and habits.

"If we can see it in our minds, we can hold it in our hands".

Bob Proctor (1934 – 2022)
Canadian Author and creator of Proctor Gallagher Institute

If we can imagine it, we are capable of having it. Through our inner world, we can live in an environment that brings us happiness, health and wealth.

Earl Nightingale once said,

"Most people tiptoe their way through life, hoping they make it safely to death."

It certainly doesn't have to be that way.

When I started to understand how my internal environment worked, I learned the importance of it. Therefore, I want to share with you how to create the life you want, whatever that may be.

My story is a lifelong journey, but one year something significant happened. It all started with a photo that my Mother took. The image was of me, and it shook me to my core. I would love to share my whole story with you, but I can only share part due to its nature. Those who know me will understand why.

My Mum was trying to capture a happy moment, but in reality, it was heartbreaking. Looking at the photo, I could feel something physically move inside my head. I can't quite explain the feeling. I was shocked, stunned, and in disbelief. My eyes couldn't, not see what I was seeing. I looked like I was dying. My hair was thin and falling out, the glands on my neck were swollen, my eyes were bloodshot, and acne covered my skin. I was pale and frail looking. I didn't recognise myself. I looked at my face every morning in the mirror, but it occurred to me that I had stopped seeing myself a long time ago. The Mayans believed a camera could capture part of your Soul in a photo. This photo showed me that my Soul was broken. That photo made me understand, like never before, that I was living in Domestic Abuse.

I had already broken up with my former partner one month previously but was still living in the same house with him. He denied we ever broke up and told me I couldn't move out. I believed him. I knew he posed a safety risk, and I needed to get out of the situation, but it didn't seem real. My Mum had even asked for his car registration in case *"something happened"*. I was depressed, and I started hating my situation. My former partner wouldn't let me practice my faith, but I found it had started to stir deep inside. I found myself thinking about the Ancient Ways, and my faith began crawling out of my mind's shadows. I started to pray for the first time in years. This spark grew into small flames, and then a fire started to burn brightly. I obsessively thought about my Tarot Cards, and I missed them. I started using them in secret when he passed out from drinking. They empowered, guided me, gave me different outcomes for various situations and, most of all, showed me my *Freedom*.

For the first time in my life, a voice that had been screaming inside my head was finally heard. All the safety measures my brain had put in place to protect itself came crashing down. The invisible bars of my prison was now visible. I lived in domestic abuse, coercive control, financial, and psychological abuse for four years. The following day I felt like I had woken up from a coma, and I started questioning my sense of reality. My mind was trying to make sense of everything. I kept asking myself, *"how did I end up here?"*. I felt like I was awake in a nightmare, that my reality didn't make sense, and then the terror set in.

Some of my memories were missing. As the day went on, the fear deepened as I frantically tried to remember past events. My stomach felt like it had a pit of snakes in it, and every time I saw him or heard his voice, they would strangle each other in a stomach-wrenching knot. I wanted to call my Mum and cry, but I was so ashamed. I was so ashamed that I let someone treat me like that. I was so ashamed that I kept secrets from them. I was so ashamed that I had lied to them to protect him. Later I learned I had been Trauma Bonded to him, but the feeling of shame lasted many months. That day I had another blow to my already battered mind. I finally understood that when the mind is sick, so is the body. For years I had tried to manage the safety of my environment. I lived on eggshells every day, was constantly in fight or flight mode, and changed my behaviour and personality in a feeble attempt to avoid his terrifying rage and outbursts of anger. All this stress, anxiety, traumas and fear had now taken its toll on my body. It was a hard lesson to accept.

I knew I had to get out, but I couldn't pack that suitcase. I was so scared of my perpetrator's anger and what he would do. For years I tried everything to keep him from getting angry, and now I was about to piss him off. He was furious when I broke up with him. I started dreaming I would end *"up dead in a ditch"*, and when I woke, I would think, *"well, at least I died trying to escape"*. I know that sounds very dramatic, but two women a week are killed by a current or former partner in England and Wales alone. One day my Mum turned up and told me I was going home with her. I didn't argue.

When I finally left, the abuse continued. When I thought things couldn't possibly get any worse, they did. I discovered there are many more layers under *"rock bottom"*. I cried more tears than I thought possible. At first, the shame didn't let me talk about the abuse, and then I went through a phase of trying to protect the ones I love from it. I thought it would utterly break their hearts to hear what my former partner had done to me. In the end, I broke and told them. To my surprise, they knew most of it. They saw it happening for years but couldn't intervene because they feared losing me. My former partner had already isolated me from most of my friends. I understand this now, but when someone is going through domestic abuse, they need to figure it out for themselves. If you tell them directly, they may not be able to accept it. My Mum had tried to have this conversation with me at the beginning of the relationship, and I didn't speak to her for two weeks. I had completely forgotten this incident.

Looking back on it, I remember saying, *"but he will change! He is under a lot of stress from work"*. There was always an excuse for his behaviour. I could not accept what she was saying because I was Trauma Bonded, a psychological response to abuse. For those of you who don't know what the term means;

"Trauma bonding is the attachment an abused person feels for their abuser, specifically in a relationship with a cyclical pattern of abuse. The bond is created due to a cycle of abuse and positive reinforcement."

Ariane Resnick

Special Diet Chef and Author

15

Some perpetrators may become very romantic to make up for their behaviour. For example, my former partner used to cook dinner and then post the pictures on social media, tagging me in them. That way, I would see all the comments about how lovely the dinner looked. The act of kindness gives the victim hope that their suffering will end and one day soon, they will receive that loving connection they so desperately need and have been promised. The suffering is also seen as a price for kindness and remorseful behaviour. The victim becomes so grateful for any acts of kindness or apologetic behaviour, no matter how small. After an incident or causing harm, an abuser may promise to change. This reinforces the Trauma Bond.

The Police were involved a month after I had left, I was allocated a Domestic Abuse Officer, and a Charity housed me. To put the cherry on the pie, my new address was leaked to my former partner in a Data Protection Breach by the Domestic Abuse Charity organising the non-molestation order. Fear saturated my cells, and there was no escape. So it was in my dreams and my waking moments. I had little to no self-esteem, my confidence was shot to pieces, and my whole world was turned upside down and inside out. I felt utterly betrayed that the agency meant to protect me, gave my former partner my new address and then blamed the incident on me.

When I had to give statements about the abuse, I had to re-live what I was trying to escape from, over and over again. I just wanted to forget, but I couldn't. I had to remember traumas in the minutest of details which entailed re-reading countless messages, reading diary entries and speaking to friends and family. The lost memories of the significant traumas were no longer lost. It all came flooding back, and again I felt nothing but shame. Shame that I forgot, and shame I let another human being treat me this way. I felt like my broken heart had been carved out and was laid bare and bleeding on a table. People became vultures, tearing off shreds of muscle and examining old scars and new wounds, all in an attempt to see how far the allegations could go. I felt so vulnerable. It felt like I had opened Pandora's box, and I could never close it again.

When I was at my lowest, I heard a little voice say, *"it's OK, it's not all been in vain"*. The voice continued, *"you have lived through the worst of it, and you are still here, you haven't ended up dead in that ditch"*. I decided that I had nothing to lose, and if I was going to go down, I was going down fighting. I found great strength in myself, and my friends and family supported me. I made a pact with myself that I didn't care if I was crawling on my knees, I wouldn't stop, and I would get through this. There was no way I would live the rest of my days like this. So, I stood tall and took on the Police Force, then the Home Secretary, my letters even made it into the Home Office. Next, I took on my Solicitors, who made a mess of my case, and the Domestic Abuse Charity, who disclosed my new address to my former partner. No more helpless victim, I was an empowered woman who was sick of being walked over. I would be heard, taken seriously and kept safe.

I started learning about the Universal Laws, went back to

university for a year and changed my mindset. I swore to myself and the Universe to share my knowledge and help others. There is no need for anyone to live a life of scarcity and fear when we can have a life full of abundance and happiness.

My life is full of happiness and abundance in all areas. This happened only when I decided to stop living in my past and use it as a platform to build from. You can set yourself free only when you know what you want. I made a decision that I am committed to *Freedom*, not suffering.

Introduction

Do you find yourself taking two steps forward, then one step backwards? Do you feel that your desires are just out of your reach? Does something come along when you have a big win and knocks you down? Do you attract one problem after the other? Do you feel your life runs the same cycles, and you can't break them?

If you have answered yes to any of these, I can help you. I deeply desire to share my knowledge to help people realise and reach their full potential, no matter where they are in their lives. I write this book sincerely hoping to elevate you to a place where dreams come true. Life is meant to be full of beautiful experiences and abundance, but for so many, life is challenging, difficult and demanding. Eighteen per cent of people live in poverty and scarcity, and sixty-three per cent of adults have personal debt. We are on the brink of a recession in 2022, with living and fuel costs experiencing all-time highs. The economy is still feeling the effects of the COVID-19 Pandemic, where one hundred and fourteen million people lost their jobs. We are experiencing a Mental Health crisis, where the young and teenagers are plagued by anxiety and depression, and older generations are also affected. A statistic that makes my heart ache is for the twelve months to the year ending March 2020. The Crime Survey for England and Wales showed that an estimated 2.3 million adults aged sixteen to seventy-four years experienced domestic abuse in the last year (1.6 million women and 757,000 men).

"To live is the rarest thing in the world. Most people exist, that is all."

Oscar Wilde (1854 – 1900)

Irish Poet

If you can relate to any of the above, you are in the right place. I know what it is like to feel the constant struggle. But I also know how incredible life can be when you change your mindset (your thoughts) and emotions (how you feel). All areas of life will change as if by Magic, and you don't need anything to do this! All you need is *you*. Yes, *you*! You are what you think, and when you add emotion to this, you reap what you sow. Imagine your mind is a garden. What seeds are you planting? When you start to look at how the mind works, your whole world will flourish. Not being a master of your mind and emotions is like a ship with no crew or captain. The ship will sink or get shipwrecked if it makes it out of the harbour! But, on the other hand, a mind with a goal is unstoppable, and mountains will move for you.

This book will help you learn the skills you need, and you will develop a deep understanding of yourself. As you work through the book, little miracles will start to occur. This inner Magic that has always belonged to you will spread into all areas of your life, and the miracles will grow as you unlock your potential. I will teach you how to become self-aware and attract more Magic. The inner workings of your mind can affect your health, wealth and happiness. When you live in love and not fear, anything is possible.

"The first step is you have to say that you can."

Will Smith (1968 -)

Actor and Singer

The beauty of this inner Magic and the skills you are about to learn is that it can help you in all areas of your life, no matter where you are. It can help you in your relationships, your career, your business, or if you are in a challenging situation.

Before we get started, there are three things you will need. The first is a journal, a lined book where you can take notes and complete some exercises. Secondly, you will need a vision board. This can be a cork board, whiteboard, piece of wood, fridge door (you can use fridge magnets) or wall where you can stick pictures too, using Blue Tac. It is going to be an area where you are going to put pictures of your dream life. If this isn't something you feel comfortable doing, you can use your journal instead. Thirdly, a piece of card or paper on which you can write your goal.

Chapter One

The Mind

We all like to think we know what is happening inside our heads. I thought I knew what was happening inside my head until I realised I hadn't the faintest idea. Many of my thoughts were on autopilot, so to speak, and I had very negative self-talk, which I didn't have the faintest idea of how to control! I look back at some moments in my life and think, *"what the Hell was I thinking?"* or *"what on Earth made me do that?"* or better yet, "where was I going with that idea?". We like to think we know ourselves, but sometimes to get to know ourselves, we need to look at things we usually ignore or hide from. The Universe works in balance, Yin and Yang, good and bad. We all have good in us and bad. I'm sure many of you have heard the saying,

"*The brightest flame casts the darkest shadow.*"

George R.R. Martin (1948 -)

American novelist

Or something similar. The Swiss psychiatrist Carl Jung (1875 – 1961) called it our *shadow selves.*

As a society, we hold no image of what the mind looks like. We all have an image of our bodies and self-image, but there is no picture of what the mind looks like. We all see in pictures, so not having a visual reference can cause confusion. To help form a clear picture of the mind, I will touch briefly on some basic psychology, and from there, we can build a mental picture.

During the 1890s and the 1930s, an Austrian neurologist, Sigmund Freud, developed the Psychodynamic Theory. Freud believed the human mind was structured into the Conscious and the Unconscious Mind, also known as the subconscious. The Conscious Mind includes everything we are aware of or things that come into our awareness. The subconscious consists of everything outside of our awareness, for example, memories, hopes, fears, motivation, traumas etc., and influences the Conscious Mind. I will speak about this in much more depth in a moment. Freud also believed that the human Psyche was made up of the; ID, Ego, and Superego, and these formed our personality. It was also acknowledged and proven with the Adverse Childhood Experiences Study (ACEs) that childhood experiences will have a monumental impact later on in adult life. This research is still very much ongoing.

It is so important to understand the effects of childhood experiences on adulthood. This research has opened up many different areas of development, including Jean Piaget placing great importance on children's education (Development Theory), John Bowlby's Attachment Theory and Anna Freud's

Play Therapy. These theories are still very much used today, for example, in our legal systems and educational systems, and are fundamental for safeguarding our children. Understanding and recognising past traumas can help with the healing process, but it can also help to understand why we are the way we are. Later in this book, I will discuss traumas and how to work through them.

"The conscious mind may be compared to a fountain playing in the sun and falling back into the great subterranean pool of subconscious from which it rises."

Sigmund Freud (1856 – 1939)

Austrian Neurologist

Conscious and Subconscious

Now that we have a basic understanding let's paint that picture. I want you to imagine your hands out in front of you. One hand is in the shape of a fist, and the other hand is open wide.

Your conscious mind is the hand that is shaped like a fist. Your conscious mind is your thinking mind, the logical Mind, the educated Mind and the intellect. Your conscious mind can accept or reject any idea and originate its own. Therefore your conscious mind is closed. However, many people have their conscious minds wide open and accept everything they see and hear. They do not understand they have the ability to control this, as they have never been taught. This lack of understanding is why we have so many mental health problems in society today, and people struggle to live in abundance in all areas of their life.

Your subconscious mind is the open hand, as it is open to everything. Your subconscious mind cannot accept or reject ideas and cannot determine what is real or imaginary. It cannot make choices, and it is not biased; it is neutral. Your subconscious mind is the emotional mind and can be linked to the Solar Plexus Chakra. I will go into much more depth about Chakras later in the book. Your subconscious mind is where the conditioning is; this can be social conditioning (peers, nursery, school etc.) or what you have seen or heard within a home environment. Our conditioning is engrained that we may not even recognise something as a learnt behaviour. These multitudes of habits control our lives and work behind the scenes controlling our every move and thought. How we are conditioned controls: our ability to earn money, our perception of ourselves and the environment around us, our use of time, our creativity, our effectiveness and productivity, and our logical mind (the conscious).

You might be asking yourself, where does this conditioning come from? Neuroscience has proved that relationships shape our brains. Human brains are not complete when they are born. Instead, they develop after birth and are literarily shaped by our experiences as a baby and child. Baby's brains grow so rapidly, that every experience they have will have a monumental impact on their later emotional capacities. As babies, our conscious mind hasn't taken shape yet, and our subconscious mind forms it. The baby's subconscious mind absorbs everything. Eighty per cent of the central neural pathways are laid, between birth and one year old. This elaborate wiring and circuiting continues, and by the age of three, nighty per cent has been laid. When we are five years old, the brain is nearly fully grown. Between the ages of two and seven, our conditioning starts to take shape, as this is when we become of ourselves as individuals.

We aren't born with fears, limitations, negative self-images, or beliefs. We are taught all of these. Our inner identity is formed through experiences of the world around us and from our role models. Now the question is, were our role models' behaviour positive or negative? How did we cope after an embarrassing experience at school or in front of family or peers? Who was there for us when we needed someone? What beliefs were we taught? What was society teaching us then, and what does it continue to teach? I learned that a woman had to have an hourglass figure, crystal clear skin, perfect make-up, and a tan. I grew up hearing that women stayed at home, but if they did work, it was in a position that cared for others, for example, a teacher, nursery practitioner, nurse or carer. They were receptionists or personal assistants if they got into an office workplace. I grew up hearing that boys don't cry; they made more money than women, brought home the money, and essentially had "male privileges". I also grew up hearing *"money doesn't grow on trees", "money is hard to earn",* and *"you live to work".* What beliefs and limitations did you grow up with? What did you see and hear as a child and into your teenage years?

Attachment Theory

To carry on from the topic of the subconscious, we will glance at the Attachment Theory, as it will help develop a better understanding of why we behave in specific ways. In addition, it is an excellent insight into how we end up where we do.

John Bowlby is a British psychologist and psychoanalyst who developed the attachment theory, which is still widely used today. It is still one of the most significant theories. However, there are now many other attachment theories which have been developed from this. The theory is based on infants' emotional development and how this is influenced by having a solid relationship with the infant's carers. Infants need a strong relationship with their carers to form an emotional connection. Their first connection should be with their Mother or a Mother figure. This connection is made through nurturing behaviour, physical contact, positive facial expressions and play. This connection will then lead the children to become confident, independent, resilient, and able to learn social skills. John Bowlby's theory underpins the Key Person System used in our nurseries, schools and childcare facilities today.

John Bowlby stressed the importance of continuous care.

Consistent relationships are vital for the growth and development of any child. They offer warmth and intimacy, and happiness. They offer protection and safety from illness and injury. They also supply the basic need of nutrition and offer a home. Children can stay calm and learn about new experiences with the help of their carers. If a child does not receive consistent care or if the attachment is broken or disrupted during the first two years, they will suffer from this for the rest of their lives. The consequences will be irreversible, and this risk will continue until they are five years old. The term for a situation like this is "maternal deprivation", and the long-term effects are depression, affectionless psychopathy (cannot show affection or concern for others), aggression, and being academically stunted.

All children need unconditional love and affection. They need someone who can understand their emotional needs, and children learn the core elements of a relationship through this understanding. As they grow, they will also learn how to manage themselves in stressful situations. Through making attachments with safe and emotionally stable caregivers, infants develop a structured means to help themselves cope with parts of their future life, they may find stressful or uncomfortable. This, in turn, will build a solid and healthy mental state and reduce anxiety. Parents who do not have this awareness and understanding may hinder their child's development.

Children need repeated experiences of being comforted so

they can develop resilience. Resilience is not just a psychological quality but a neurological and physiological one. I have already stated that neuroscience has proved that relationships shape our brains. Every child's experience will significantly impact their later emotional capacities. So, what does this look like in adulthood? In adulthood, the person may find themselves not able to self-regulate their feelings, they would not be able to manage their stressors, and they would not be aware of their emotional processes. Some people may not be able to deal with the emotional pressures of daily life and would turn to alcohol and substance abuse.

Childhood emotions have a long-lasting biological impact, as outlined in the ground-breaking Adverse Childhood Experiences Study (ACEs). Abuse or neglect of any kind directly affects health problems in adulthood. Children can experience emotional distress if they do not have a reliable warm relationship to turn to when they feel anxious. Children who appear to have ADHD may be dealing with Childhood Traumas or Abuse, as Trauma and ADHD look very similar. Hyper-vigilance is often a response to trauma, as it is the elevated state of constantly assessing potential threats; essentially, it is fight or flight mode.

Some of you reading this may worry about your upbringing or perhaps how you raise your children. It is not only childhood traumas that can cause problems, but traumas that happen later in life. If you have been through traumas yourself, please don't worry, there is hope for you yet. We will explore how to move past these later, and there is light at the end of the tunnel. With this new knowledge, change can start to happen within our minds. Self-awareness is one of the greatest keys to success in all areas of life. Self-awareness can bring wealth, positive, healthy relationships, good health, and much more. As a Being, we are constantly evolving; we never stop. The only constant in the Universe is change. Through self-awareness and healing, we can move some of these blockages and walls that hold us back.

The Power of You

Now we have a much better understanding of the mind, let's have some fun. We can re-condition ourselves. We can rewrite this programming that is holding us back and excel at everything in life. You do not have to live life how you have been told to!

There are many different forms of counselling, but I love the Humanistic approach. While studying, I learnt about the founder of the humanistic approach, Carl Rogers. Rogers initially looked at the Freudian method, as this was the first of the *"talking cures"*, but was inspired by Otto Rank and moved away from this. His name appears alongside the term person-centred approach, where a person is seen to have sufficient resources to deal with any problem life throws at them. I do not believe this is the case, and I know it is. You only need *you* and your beautiful mind. But, as Carl Rogers did, I believe people have forgotten or are denied these skills.

We are all unique individuals, and our experiences are unique; therefore, *we* can work through them because *we* experienced them. With the right conditions, people can grow and become whole. We can develop our personalities and emotional maturity through self-development and learning about self-importance. We know that our concept of self changes by being influenced by other people's opinions and expectations. The more self-aware we become, the more we can control this for the better. When we are faced with a crisis, we come to question who we are. This crisis could be in any area of our lives. My crisis realised that I was in domestic abuse, which was my turning point. I surrounded myself with a support network and worked through the process. No one else could do it for me, and I had to. I learnt that I had the tools to deal with anything, and this tool was my mind.

Many people struggle with their "*real self*" and believe their "*outer self*" is who they are. To progress and excel, you must be who you want to be. Not who your Mum or Dad wants you to be, not who your husband or wife wants you to be, not who your children want you to be, not who your peers want you to be. By getting in touch with your true feelings, ideas and values and becoming the person you want to be, you start living the Magic. It is by human design to want to grow and thrive. You need to find your desire to develop spiritually, emotionally, creatively and physically. Then, you have the tools to deal effectively with the problems you will face in your life. If you want others to respect, love and honour you, then you need to respect, love and honour yourself first. If you don't, you can't expect others to.

"People are just as wonderful as sunsets if I can let them be. When I look at a sunset, I don't find myself saying, "Soften the orange a little on the right-hand corner, and put a bit more purple along the base, and use a little more pink in the cloud colour." I don't do that. I don't try to control a sunset. I watch it with awe as it unfolds."

Carl Rogers (1902 – 1987)
American Psychologist

Linking Mind and Body

When I started learning that we could rewrite our brains, were what we thought, and could create anything we desired, my question was, *"but how?"*. How does this work on a science level? How does this physically work? I have faith, but I needed more.

The magnificent tools that we have are our Mind and Body. We care so much for things we have to purchase, but we care so little for items that are freely given to us, our Minds and our Body. Our beautiful tools are connected to a third entity. The third one has many names, the Divine energy source, God, Goddess, Mother Earth, Father Green, and The Universe.

Whatever your faith is, there is a power greater than our own, an infinite source of energy where everything came from.

Now let's talk about the power of our subconscious mind. But first, let's talk about Science and Magic and allow us to begin seeing and understanding the beauty of it. The subconscious and conscious minds have their own nervous systems, which gradually link together in the body.

To simplify things:

Conscious Mind:

- This works in the cerebrospinal or voluntary system

- This system is linked to your senses and the voluntary movements of your body

- The control centre for this is in the cerebral cortex in the brain

- Your conscious mind is your reasoning mind, and it makes choices. For example, it chooses your partners, your favourite colour, what to wear, and how your house looks.

- Your conscious mind is your rational mind or objective mind. Your conscious mind deals with the environment and objective World through your five senses.

- Whatever you think about will sink into your subconscious mind, good or bad, positive or destructive, and this will be accepted without question.

- Through the use of Prayer, you can influence your subconscious mind.

- Your conscious mind never could do the job your subconscious mind does in operating your body.

- Worry, depression, stress, fear and anxiety can affect your heart, lungs, stomach and intestines. The medical community is now recognising mental health's effects on the body. Remember the lesson I spoke of earlier? When the mind is sick, so is the body.

Subconscious mind:

- This works in the autonomic system or involuntary nervous system.

- This works in several areas, including the cerebellum, brain stem and the amygdala.

- Our subconscious mind also works in an area called our *"second brain"*, a large complex structure of nerves located in our abdominal area, also known as the Celiac (Solar) Plexus area. This *"second brain"* contains more neurons than the spinal cord or the peripheral nervous system.

- Your subconscious controls your heartbeat, digestion, circulation, vital functioning, and breathing. It can transform food into blood, bone and muscle tissue. It does this twenty-four hours a day, seven days a week. It never stops.

- You would have felt this *"second brain"* speaking to you but probably did not realise it. It speaks to us through feelings, though having *"butterflies"* in your stomach, through that *"gut feeling"* of intuition. These feelings are our subconscious mind communicating with the conscious mind.

- Now you understand that your second brain contains some hundred million neurons, how seriously will you start taking its messages?

- Your subconscious is your creative or subjective mind and draws on an infinite power and wisdom that resides in you. It has the power of clairvoyance and can collect information through divine sources. When your conscious mind is quiet, your subconscious mind performs at its best.

- Remember, we are souls in a body, not a body with a soul attached.

- Unlike the conscious mind, the subconscious mind never sleeps and never rests. You can tap into this infinite power by speaking to it before you sleep. Your subconscious will talk back to you through your dreams.

Both of these organs have their own connections to our

significant systems and vital functions of the body. They can work separately or synchronously; for example, our bodies may respond to danger before consciously noticing the perceived threat. Our thoughts and ideas are electrical currents, and when we have a thought, a parallel current is produced in our involuntary nervous system. This is how our conscious mind speaks to our subconscious mind. Let's remember your subconscious mind cannot accept or reject ideas and cannot determine between what is real or imaginary. Your subconscious mind believes whatever your conscious mind tells it. Your subconscious mind will carry out instructions no matter what they are. Sometimes things will happen straight away; sometimes, they will take time.

I will give you an example. In September, I decided I wanted compensation money for the data protection breach of my personal information. I *"felt"* this was the sum for me. I had thought about it for days, and the feeling grew. I decided to take action, and I involved a solicitor and started down the legal route. I was told it would take between three to six months to resolve. The Domestic Abuse Charity dragged its feet and ignored the solicitors. So, on the second of February the following year, I complained to the Information Commissioners Office (ICO). I never gave up, and in fact, my faith grew. Like I never knew before, I would have that money. In July, I finally received an email from the ICO, and they started investigating. I had a meeting with a barrister (I had waited ten months for this meeting because of the deliberate delays caused by the charity), and I kept on praying. I had negative self-talk in my head because everything was taking so long. The self-talk was telling me I wasn't worthy of that money, telling me it wasn't meant to be because it was taking too long, telling me I didn't have a case, telling me I would lose, telling me to give up. I felt terrible I was *"taking"* from a Charity. I mean, how could I? Other victims needed those resources that the money I was *"taking"* would pay for. I mean, who sues a charity?

This was my conditioning talking. I fought it. I told it to move aside because I was in the driver's seat, and that money *was* mine! I even bought Prosecco and stuck a check from the Universe on it (The Secret Check from thesecret.tv). I told my toddler we were going on holiday, and I planned how to use the money to set up multiple sources of income. I told people I was winning the case! People thought I was crazy. Every time I had a doubt, I replaced it with prayer. Every time I had negative self-talk, I replaced it with prayer. And what is prayer? Prayer is *desire*. Some people only pray in times of crisis, but to pray effectively, prayer should be done in times of *plenty*! Many other obstacles were thrown my way, but I overcame them. Prayer helped me with my mental health, as the victim blaming the Charity was doing was psychologically very damaging. The case was still not resolved at the time of writing this book. In the end, I decided to involve my local MP and take it even further. The challenges strengthened my faith and my belief. Think negatively, and the outcome will be negative; think positively, and the result will be positive. The Laws of the

Universe also come into play here, and I will discuss those later. I truly believed the outcome would be positive.

How did prayer help? So here is the Secret. Here is the discovery of the century that has always been known. It doesn't matter what *you* believe in, it matters what *your* subconscious mind believes in. Because your subconscious mind has the *power* to make it comes true. Your power makes your subconscious believe in what you want to be true. When we convey a thought to our subconscious mind, it imprints on a brain cell. Your subconscious mind then works to make this thought come true. If you wake up in the morning and say, with feeling, *"I'm going to have a bad day"*, you *will* have a bad day because your subconscious mind essentially says, "your wish is my command". If you wake up and say, "*I'm going to have a fantastic day"*, you will have a fantastic day! Your subconscious doesn't know the difference between a good and bad feeling; it creates more of that feeling.

Dreams

I briefly touched on dreams above. Let's dive into them in more detail. Freud made a breakthrough in dream analysis, theorising that dreams were a link to our subconscious mind. He thought that if you could understand your dreams, you could solve problems you faced in life. Dream analysis is still very much used today, and Freud used dream analysis to start his method of Free Associations. Many great minds have solved problems through their dreams. You have the ability to do this.

Take a look at the world around you. Everything was invented. Everything started as an idea in someone else's conscious mind. Or, in some cases, a dream. I want you to start taking notes of your dreams. If you don't remember them on waking, put the intention in your subconscious mind before you sleep that you will remember them on waking. Write these down in your journal or another notebook if you wish. Salvador Dali painted his dreams onto canvas in the most breath-taking way.

Who doesn't love Google? If Larry Page hadn't had a nightmare triggered by anxiety, we probably wouldn't have Google today. Larry dreamt he could download the whole internet onto some old computers. Why did he dream this? It turns out he feared not being accepted into Stamford University by mistake. When Larry woke up, he started to work on the maths equations and soon discovered the idea was all right. So Google was born two years later. Dr James Watson dreamt of a spiral staircase in 1953 and designed the double helix spiral structure for our DNA. Elias Howe dreamt in 1845 that he was captured by cannibals who stabbed him repeatedly with spears that had a hole in the tip. What invention was born out of this dream? The humble sewing machine. Elias Howe realised you needed an eye in the needle tip to create the lock-stitch sewing machine. He had been working on this invention for a while and figured it out from his slightly morbid dream. Einstein came up with the Theory of Relativity in his dream. You are probably wondering what on Earth his dream must have been about! He dreamt he was with a farmer and a herd of cows huddled up against a fence. The farmer turned the electric fence on, and the cows jumped back. Einstein and the farmer both saw the cows jump back, but in different ways, and this is what inspired Einstein. Events look different from different angles because the light reaches your eyes at different times. Frankenstein, The Periodic Table, The Structure of The Atom, Dr Frederick Banting solved the problem of Diabetes, and yes, even The Terminator film all came from dreams.

We are infinite divine beings. We can tap into unlimited powers when we engage our subconscious mind. Here is a personal example. When I was pregnant, I was in survival mode. My unborn child was my whole world, and I wanted nothing more than to keep him safe. So, my subconscious went into safety mode and spoke to me through dreams to keep me safe. This is how, when I was three months pregnant (December 2019), I had a recurring nightmare that I was in labour, walking down a street somewhere. I was panicking because I was alone and worried I wouldn't make it to the hospital on time. But there was something else to worry about too. A Zombie Virus had taken over the world, and there were Zombies everywhere. I was surrounded by the dead, and everything I knew and loved was gone. The whole world was burning (literally), and I was standing there in a white T-shirt and shorts, about to give birth. My beautiful son was born at the beginning of June 2020 at the height of the COVID-19 Pandemic. I had to go to the hospital alone because of restrictions and the lockdown, and I wore a white T-shirt and maternity shorts. The whole world seemed to have changed overnight, and millions tragically died. When I reflect on this dream, I see how it was a warning of things to come.

My dreams have given me so much insight into court cases that I am currently going through, dealings with the Police, and my dating life, and my dreams have also played a big part in writing this book.

Sleep is a Divine Law

My beautiful son didn't use to sleep very well. I am a single full-time Mum, twenty-four hours a day, seven days a week, and I remember being at the point where I just wanted to cry. If I'm honest, I did a lot! I was so resentful to hear other parents complain about how their child disturbed their sleep one night or woke up earlier than usual. I used to think, *"what the Hell are they complaining about? And there are two of them!"* When you are on your own nothing is easy, there is double the workload, and you have to be the: Mum, Dad, peacemaker, have boundaries in place (good cop – bad cop type of thing), homemaker, breadwinner and juggle all of life's other problems. Harrison used to wake up every two hours since the day he was born. He wouldn't sleep longer than an hour during the day, he went to bed from eight pm onwards and was up without question at four am. This situation went on for two years. So you begin to understand very quickly why sleep deprivation is used as a form of torture. Some nights I was lucky to get four hours of sleep, which affected my emotional well-being.

Sleep deprivation can cause depression, irritability, mood swings, and in some cases, psychotic breakdown. You need sleep to have a life full of joy, happiness and abundance. When you sleep, you recharge spiritually, which is very important. It is a common belief that the body needs sleep, but this isn't the case. Nothing rests while you are asleep. Your heart doesn't stop beating, your lungs don't stop breathing, your stomach doesn't stop digesting food, your skin still sweats, your hair and nails still grow, and your body's vital functions do not stop. Your subconscious mind never stops. We heal quicker when we are asleep because our conscious mind doesn't get in the way of our subconscious mind. Our conscious mind needs a break from the sensory world around us and the confusion and noise. We also *need* to dream, and this is why we sleep.

Every human, animal and plant sleeps, it is a Divine Law. Everyone needs, on average, eight hours or more sleep a night. If you are lucky enough to get this, you spend one-third of your life asleep. That's, on average, twenty-five years of dreaming. There are five stages of sleep, and the first four are called non-R.E.M. (Rapid Eye Movement) sleep. These stages of sleep are characterised as thoughts rather than dreams. The fifth stage of sleep is where vivid dreaming starts to happen. It is called the REM stage of sleep and is a paradox stage. Even though we are in a deep stage of sleep, our brainwaves show alertness, our adrenal glands secrete adrenaline, so we are ready for action, and our muscles twitch. However, our body is heavy and limp and oblivious to external stimuli. Unless you are a Mum, this is, as we form something called a "protection reflex" in our brains. The protection reflex develops when you become a Mother, and essentially it means you instantly wake up if your baby so much as snuffles in their sleep. Or you might wake up a few moments before your baby or child does, and then they wake. I can still vividly remember falling out of bed because Harrison let out a cry during the night. I would run to his crib, exhausted, disorientated, nauseous from the lack of sleep, and shaking from the adrenalin rush. The minute my head would hit the pillow, I was off dreaming again. Scientists have proved there is a need to dream. For every hundred minutes of sleep, we experience seventy to ninety minutes of non-R.E.M. sleep, and then we drift into a deeper R.E.M. sleep cycle for around ten to twenty minutes. Scientists have discovered that if we are repeatedly woken up during the R.E.M. stage of sleep, we compensate by having an extended period of R.E.M. sleep when we are allowed to sleep.

Dream Exercise

Task one: In your Journal, I want you to document your dreams. Try and do this the minute you wake up, as they will be fresh in your mind. Being a parent, I know this might be an impossible task. You don't get a minute to think when your child wakes up screaming first thing in the morning or during the night, let alone write in a journal. However, there is a way. When there is a *will*, there is a *way*. I use my voice-note app on my phone. I hit the record button and spoke my dream out loud while sorting out Harrison. I describe it in as much detail as I can, then write it down later. I say anything unsuitable in the dream for young ears in a coded way. The voice-note facility is terrific, and I use it for everything.

Task two: If you have any problems in life for which you need guidance, write them in your journal and speak them aloud or in your mind before falling asleep. Your subconscious will give you the answers. If you are in a relationship, talk to them about it, and then both of you can ask your subconscious for help and guidance. You might have children who are old enough to understand who could join in. If the problem is a family problem, involve the family in an age-appropriate way. By teaching your children, you are teaching them valuable life skills and teaching them they can achieve and obtain anything they want. You may want to work through it yourself if it is a personal problem.

Before you go to sleep, still your mind and body, breathe deeply and relax. Breathe in for five seconds and out for eight seconds. Repeat this three times. Feel your body relax, and your thoughts settle. Thoughts and feelings are the actions, and the results you receive from your subconscious mind are the reactions (The Law of Cause and Effect). Feeling happy when you are seeking an answer or a solution to a problem is essential. Ask your subconscious for help, like you would a loved one. Speak to your subconscious as if it were the most loving person in the world, who just wanted to help you, and the best outcome for you. Think about how happy you would be for the perfect solution or answer. I want you to *feel* how glad you would be if you had all the answers you seek now. Let your mind play with these happy emotions of relief, love, joy and gratitude. Finally, fall asleep in a relaxed, content way.

In the next chapter, I will speak about the Universal Laws, and you will see how quickly you will start to use them to make a big difference in your life.

Your subconscious mind will speak to you through feelings, inner awareness, or a hunch. For example, you might be having a conversation with someone, and then suddenly, the answer pops into your head out of the blue. You might even pick up a magazine or newspaper, and the answer is in the headlines. Whatever the method, the answer will come to you in divine timing.

If you are like me, you are asleep the minute your head hits the pillow. Using the different Laws, I managed to get my little boy to sleep through the night. However, the four am wake-ups never relented. By the end of the day, I was exhausted after being up at four am. Harrison is a hyperactive little thing, and it takes him an hour to fall asleep at night, and we hadn't mastered self-settling at the time of writing this book. So, I started putting some headphones on after reading his bedtime story and listening to some relaxing music. In my mind, I would speak to my subconscious in a relaxed state. I would spend an hour daydreaming about the best possible outcome for a problem, or I would go over my goal list. Staying calm and relaxed was challenging, especially when your toddler wanted to get out of bed and run laps around the room. But, through sheer persistence, I would prevail. I would make sure he could hear me breathing in and out, slowly and steadily, and soon enough, he started to copy. Sitting in a relaxed state rubbed off onto him, and he began to calm down a lot quicker.

The energy and frequency I was emitting balanced his. Earlier, I mentioned the name Jean Piaget; his theory and Stages of Cognitive Development prove that children learn by copying behaviour. Showing your child/ren how to settle through breathing techniques is teaching them an essential skill. They can use this breathing technique and stillness to regulate themselves emotionally. In an age-appropriate way, you can teach them what you are doing. Ask them to lie in their beds and prepare for sleep, but before they do, get them to engage with their subconscious mind. They could imagine the perfect outcome for their SATs, find the perfect best friend, find the perfect pet, experience an unforgettable family holiday, learn how to engage with their inner wisdom, and become confident, well-rounded individuals. Imagine the effectiveness of this technique in their teenage years when they might be trying to. Resolve a friendship dispute, study for exams, look for a part-time job, look for the perfect boyfriend/girlfriend etc. When preparing for bed, I would relax my body (you don't need to be sitting still to do this) and tap into my subconscious mind again. When I lay down, I held onto the thought that I had already had the required conversation and would receive the desired information. In the morning, I would start talking to my voice recorder. Whatever works for you, you will find a way.

Chapter Two

Universal Laws

We will work with some Kybalion Universal Laws throughout this book. It would be easier to explain them in one chapter and incorporate them as I go along. This way, all the information is in one place, and you can return to this chapter anytime. The more you develop emotionally and spiritually, the more all of this will make sense. It might benefit you to read this chapter a few times, as your understanding will grow each time you read it. When you understand the laws at play in the Universe are *constantly* working with us, you will see how to work in harmony with them.

There are some prominent theories and concepts in this chapter. When I learnt about them, I rejected some at first. The more I developed myself, the more I accepted. Some things were pretty hard to swallow and didn't sit well. Why? Because life can be so damn hard, and I couldn't believe I was making life happen; life wasn't happening to me. I then worked through the layers and questioned why I rejected some of the Universal Laws. The answer I found was fear and old conditioning, and I had yet to discover the true meaning of forgiveness. When this all started to change, everything just clicked together.

So, what are the Universal Laws? First, there are natural laws, such as gravity, that keep everything physical in order. Then there are Universal Laws or Principals which govern the entire Universe. These Universal Laws have been taught for centuries and date as far back as Ancient Egypt to Ancient Greece and Ancient India. The Kybalion speaks of these Laws and is based on the Ancient Hermetic teachings, which were first published in 1908. I will be using The Kybalion teachings when referring to the Universal Laws.

"Everything is dual; everything has poles; everything has its pair of opposites; like and unlike are the same; opposites are identical in nature, but different in degree; extremes meet; all truths are but half-truths; all paradoxes may be reconciled."

The Kybalion

A Study of the Hermetic Philosophy

The Law of Mentalism

"The All is Mind-

- *the Universe is Mental"*

The Kybalion

A Study of the Hermetic Philosophy

We are all one. We are all connected to one Source. This

concept might be hard to comprehend as we very much like to think of ourselves as individuals. We are all individuals with our own very unique Soul Signature/Energy Signature/Vibration, but our Soul is connected to a greater Source. Some call this Source the Divine, the Universe, God, or the Great Spirit. But essentially, they are all the same thing.

As the English Poet, John Donne (1572 – 1631) would say,

"No Man Is an Island."

This idea might be hard to wrap your head around, but follow me for a bit. Quantum physics teaches us that thought must proceed first for anything to exist. So what does this mean? It means the Universe cannot exist without a conscious mind entering into it. The famous John Archibald Wheeler (1911 – 2008) was an American theoretical physicist and colleague of Albert Einstein (1879 – 1955) and Niels Bohr (1885 – 1962) who supported this theory. He stated that the Universe and the observer exist as a pair; without this coupling, nothing could exist. Through this principle, it is believed that this Source, the Divine, the Universe, God, or the Great Spirit (whatever you call it) is consciousness or thoughts, and our reality is a manifestation of this Greater Mind. It is also believed that we are created in the image of God. If we are made in the image of God, we can create anything we desire because we have the power of God. By understanding the Universe's Natural Laws, we can harness this power and create any life we want.

To sum up, our entire Universe is a product of your conscious and subconscious thoughts and emotions. By learning how to use the power of our Mind, Body and Spirit, we can manifest the life of our dreams. We can start to create an environment where anything is possible, and miracles will come flooding in. All the guidance, support and knowledge you need will be at your fingertips. You can impress your desires on the Universe, and your subconscious mind will manifest them into physical form.

Now that you understand we all come from the same *"pool"*, so to speak, you will start seeing people differently. You will see how we are truly equal; our attitude and perspective set us apart. You will also begin to understand why you are where you are at this moment in time. We all have this amazing ability to tap into this unlimited power. We each have our own frequency, and depending on this frequency, we attract like-for-like. Fear is the lowest frequency, and love is the highest frequency. Live a life of fear, and you will attract more of those frightening experiences. I lived in a fear-based environment for four years while experiencing domestic abuse. When I found the meaning of love through a life-changing experience, it filled my whole being with unconditional love, and my frequency changed. After four months, I broke free from the abuse, and my external environment shifted to match my internal environment. However, I still had a life with plenty of fear. But, I was going through Quantum Leap after Quantum Leap, and my frequency was constantly changing. I will go into much more detail about Quantum Leaps later in the book.

Understanding that you can create anything you desire is like being handed a catalogue for the Universe or a menu. It is like going into the biggest superstore imaginable and being told you can have anything you want, and the currency is frequency. Match the frequency, and it is yours. As we work through this book, you will learn the fantastic tools to help you learn how to tap into this infinite divine source. You will learn how to attract; health, happiness, money, dream career, relationships, personal desires and material items.

It is important to remember that the Universe works in balance. I'm sure you look at some people and envy their lives. Things seem to come so quickly to them, and they appear to float through life with no apparent problems. However, it's important to remember that they will experience their highs and lows, and we are all equal. We all experience good and bad days no matter where we are in life. The difference here is *how* you deal with those bad days. In this book, you will learn how to believe in yourself, trust yourself, and go from thinking that you're not enough to knowing that you're more than enough to create the life you want.

"You live inside this omnipresent mind of all... the entire Universe (including yourself and your life) is composed of an all-encompassing Divine mind, its thoughts, and thought form.... Your true mind (your Higher Self) is an extension and a creation of the Divine Mind."

Doreen Virtue (1958 -)

American Author and Motivational Speaker

The Law of Vibration

"Nothing rests;

* *everything moves;*

* *everything vibrates"*

The Kybalion

A Study of the Hermetic Philosophy

The Law of Vibration has a secondary law called The Law of Attraction. I will speak about this Law separately, but they are very much interlinked.

As spoken about before, we all have our unique vibrations. Everything in existence has its own unique vibration. The Universe is in constant movement right down to atoms and molecules vibrating. We are in continuous motion too. When you hold your hand up in front of you, the atoms are moving so quickly they appear to be still. Molecules and atoms moving emit a frequency.

Everything in our life right now is something we have attracted. It can almost sound like a cruel joke, but like attracts like. The frequency we are emitting is attracting more of the same. I will give you a physical example of vibration and frequency; if you hit a tuning fork with a hammer, it will cause other tuning forks in the vicinity to vibrate at the same frequency and simultaneously. Dowsing rods can tune into the frequency, too, and these can be used to detect water, metals and other objects.

Our thoughts (frequency) and feelings (vibrations) attract more of the same into our lives and have been taught over the centuries. It is why I would never Hex anyone, as sending harm to someone only causes the harm to return to myself. Karma is another example; your actions, work, or deeds will have an effect or consequence on yourself. For instance, if your thoughts are of joy, love, gratitude and happiness, then the Universe will send you situations, opportunities and people corresponding with how you feel.

Putting different methods into practice can attract more of the same frequency and raise your vibrational frequency. Remember, fear is a low frequency, and love is the highest. To start attracting what you want in life, you need to put that frequency out to the Universe to attract more. Imagine you are a tuning fork and want to directly attract circumstances, opportunities, people and money into your life. Vibrating at a higher frequency will attract more of what you want into your life. We are magnetic beings; we don't need to do anything to become more magnetic; we are made in the image of God. We need to fine-tune the life we want.

The Law of Attraction

Our thoughts (frequency) and feelings (vibrations) attract more of the same into our lives. Using this deliberately through meditations, affirmations, visualisation and Prayer to create a frequency is essentially the Law of Attraction.

Many people have watched the film *The Secret* or read both books (*The Secret* and *The Magic*) and have had little or no success manifesting their desires. It is easy for people to say, *"think positive and positive miracles will follow"*. I'm not the type of motivational speaker who says, *"think positive"* all the time. We are human and complex beings with different unique experiences, and thinking positively isn't an easy task sometimes. Many people try and manifest their desires from fear. For example, they want to earn more, to avoid or get out of debt. This desire to earn more comes from a place of fear. The fear is debt and scarcity, and this frequency attracts more. If you want to earn more to buy your dream home, buy a new car, or go on an unforgettable holiday, the desire comes from wanting something that brings you joy. The thought of a new home, new car or holiday excites you and gets you dreaming about all the lovely things that go with those desires. If you see something in your mind, you can hold it in your hands. You can attract your desires by changing your vibrations. Feelings are the conscious awareness of vibrations. We are what we think, and this knowledge brings so much power.

"The Law of Attraction allows for infinite possibilities, infinite abundance, and infinite joy. It knows no order of difficulty, and it can change your life in every way if you let it."

Jack Canfield (1944 -)

American Author, Motivational Speaker, Corporate Trainer, and Entrepreneur

Now flipping the fear switch over to joy can take some work. It should not feel hard or a constant struggle. It should feel harmonious and balanced because you will receive struggle in return if you fight it. It's perfectly OK to have bad days, experience those feelings, and work *through* them. Never bury them and put on a fake smile. The Universe knows all, and you can't cheat yourself. I also want to point out we don't *"get rid"* of emotions. Energy cannot be created or destroyed. We change our negative emotions into positive ones. When we don't work through our emotions we don't have spaciousness. We need spaciousness to nurture our negative emotions, and change them to positive ones. We cannot do this work if there is too much clutter, so to speak.

How do you flip the fear switch without that internal struggle? It is all about perspective. Your perspective is critical to changing your mindset, and we need to change your mindset to start attracting more of what you want.

We all want something.

And

We are all afraid of something.

Stop thinking about what it is you fear, as you are giving it your power and manifesting your fears into reality. Take your power back and start giving your dreams your power. Please start thinking about what you want, and your dreams will manifest into reality.

"To let life happen to you is irresponsible. To create your day is your divine right."

Ramtha

Spiritual Entity channelled by Judy Zebra "J. Z." Knight (1946 -)

The Law of Inspired Action

When the Divine speaks to us, or our subconscious, it does so through feelings. That inner gut instinct, that intuition, that urge or hunch. When we feel any of these pulls, we must go with them. They are the Divine speaking through your subconscious mind and into your conscious mind.

It is not enough to desire something. We need to have a burning desire! To constructively use the Law of Attraction, we must take Inspired Action. We need Goals.

When I left my former abusive partner, I questioned my whole reality. He told me I imagined the abuse. I had memory loss, and my brain struggled to retain information and I was being gaslighted. I could have looked at my current situation and doomed myself to believing my current state was my future state. Don't look at where you are now and believe this is your future. It isn't, and it is just a phase. Don't let your past and present surround you and create your future. Stand on your past and use it as a platform to begin a new one. Your future is not made tomorrow. It is made today.

How did I escape my life of Hell? First, I created goals to coincide with my burning desires. I desired freedom and a new life of abundance, health, wealth and happiness. This is where Inspired Action came into play. As I discovered my infinite emotional intelligence, I was attracting different situations, events and people into my life, but I had to take action! This is how I met Michaela Chapman, Vickie J Parris, and Jax Emilio Robinson, whom I hold very dear.

Stay calm if you miss the boat the first time. The Divine will send you the opportunity again, but it may take time. I did this *twice* and finally accepted the offer on the third round. The point is on the third go, I had faith and trust and went for it. I was offered to join the Freedom Era, and my old thought processes got in the way. I had attracted this fantastic opportunity into my life, but I hesitated and missed it. The Divine offered it *again*, and I hesitated and missed it. The third time I dove right in and have never regretted it. I was so fortunate, but then I believed "what is meant to be, will be". My hesitation was a lesson to learn from. Taking action was a lesson to learn from. The

Freedom Era, created by Jax Emilio Robinson, has offered me more than financial Freedom. It has taught me everything about authentic personal branding and leveraging social media to create a thriving online income. I have attracted so many like-minded souls into my life who have empowered me to make more Freedom of choice and time. It becomes easier to start trusting that gut feeling and taking Inspired Action. You begin seeing beautiful results, giving you more faith and burning desires. We need to stretch ourselves to grow.

Remember, you are the only problem and the only solution. Our body is an instrument to our minds, and when our body moves into action, it produces results. All your dreams are on the other side of your fear; facing your fear brings them death. This is Inspired Action.

The Law of Relativity

Your first thought may have been of Einstein when you saw this Law. Everything we see, experience or feel, we attach a meaning to. This Law applies not only to yourself but to everyone around you. For example, my Mum had an experience in school as a child where she was force-fed a carrot by the dinner lady one lunchtime. She has never eaten a carrot since. Every time she sees a carrot, she thinks of that dinner lady. She has attached her own emotion and experience to carrots.

In the past, I used to think carrots helped you see in the dark.

I'm sure many of you can guess why. As a child, to eat my vegetables, my parents used to tell us stories to encourage us to eat our greens. For example, if you eat sweetcorn, you will grow tall like a giant; if you eat carrots, you can see in the dark. The Air Ministry began the story of carrots in World War II. To prevent the Germans from finding out the British were using radar and intercepting bombers, they issued press releases stating that British pilots were eating lots of carrots, giving them exceptional night vision. People believed it!

When I think of carrots, I think of dreams and time frames. I was watering some carrots I was growing in the garden with Harrison, my son. I looked at them and wanted to know how long it takes for carrots to grow. It felt like they were taking forever. It takes seventy to eighty days for a carrot to grow; some can take up to one hundred days. Yes, it takes one hundred days to produce a carrot. This got me thinking, how many of us give up on our dreams because we don't see instant results or think it has *"failed"*? Do we give our Goals and Dreams one hundred days to grow? Or do we pack it in the first couple of weeks? If a carrot gets up to one hundred days to grow, your Dreams are worthy of that too! So I decided to give myself the goal of writing a book in ninety days. I told myself I would succeed. I knew I would. I stuck it on my Goal board and carried it with me on my Goal Card, which is now permanently attached to my phone. Every time I look at my phone, I read my goal. I knew if I believed it and connected an emotional response to that belief, then Universal Law would make it happen. Whenever I see a carrot, I think of this experience and revelation.

A carrot is. A carrot is not a distant memory of being force-fed, a carrot is not the answer to exceptional night vision, and a carrot is not the answer to writing a book in a specific time frame. A carrot just is. Like a negative situation, negative is only relative to the meaning you attach to it. So when we realise everything just is, it is incredibly empowering.

We are the ones who attach meaning to situations, people, animals, insects or things, and everyone else attaches their meanings. It is like a personal filter on the world around us. To understand this is where the power lies.

The Law of Correspondence

As above, so below;

- *"As above, so below, as within, so without, as the Universe, so the soul."*

Hermes Trismegistus

Legendary Hellenistic Figure

The Celts worshipped the trees and felt an intrinsic connection with their surroundings, so for this Law, it is only appropriate to tell you the Oak Tree story. The following paragraphs will refer to various parts of trees as metaphors for spiritual growth. The Celts delved deeply into Nature for answers to the secrets of life, and with these soulful connections, they discovered a pearl of deep wisdom.

The Oak Tree, The King of Trees, is also known as the Tree of Life and is elegantly illustrated in a Celtic Knot Work style. This motif represents The Law of Correspondence. The word "Oak" also means "door" and is linked to new opportunities, seeing both sides of the picture, and has associations with strength, wisdom and endurance.

The Tree of Life design has an interweaving pattern of branches identical to the root system. The roots of the Oak tree mirror the size of the branches above ground, embodying the famous wisdom from Hermes Trismegistus, "As Above, So Below". To understand this statement is to truly experience the broader connectivity of thought, manifestation and the cycles of life.

The Oak tree is a visual reference to understanding how the unseen roots mirror the seen system of the branches above. It demonstrates the importance and correlations between life's seen and unseen aspects.

Here are a few examples to help you understand further:

- The condition of the mind (unseen) affects physical health (I learnt from Domestic Abuse a sick mind means a sick body)

- The state of your spiritual life (unseen) affects physical health

- Our beliefs (unseen – our root system, paradigm) feed and control our daily life (visible consequences, actions, results)

- Our thoughts (above/unseen) are directly connected to manifestation (below/seen). Think about the Law of Attraction and The Law of Vibration. We attract like for like, and our thoughts (internal) create/mirror our external environment.

From these examples, we then see how "everything is connected", and through small changes like prayer, meditation, and affirmations, our inner (unseen) environment can change our external (seen) environment as they mirror each other. Remember, *"as the Universe, so the soul";* we are all unique expressions of the Universe. The Universe cannot exist without a Mind entering into it. We manifest our world through the perception of life. The roots of an Oak tree grow deep into the Earth; within us, we, too, have a deep wisdom that resides deep within us. A tree cannot grow tall unless the roots grow deep; we cannot raise our frequencies unless we are grounded.

The Law of Rhythm

"Everything flows, out and in;

- *everything has its tides;*

- *all things rise and fall;*

- *the pendulum-swing manifests in everything:*

- *the measure of the swing to the right is the measure of the swing to the left;*

- *rhythm compensates"*

The Kybalion

A Study of the Hermetic Philosophy

It is easy to see this Law in action everywhere around us. There is the day and the night, the tide coming in and out, the season changing, and the planets going retrograde. We all have our highs, and we all have our lows; we have happy moments and sad moments, and we all have good days and bad days.

If you think of your mind as a garden, and your thoughts are your seeds, what you plant will manifest into reality. There are days for sowing and days for reaping. Most of the time, people see only the reaping in someone else's life, they do not see behind the scenes, and they do not see the sowing. They do not see the investment people make in themselves or the time and effort to keep everything harmonious. It is so easy to look at another and feel jealousy, envy, resentment and to judge. Remember, these are the lowest frequencies; feeling them will only attract more of the negative into your life.

There will be times in your life when you need to ask for help, and there will be times when you will give help. This *"phase"* in your life is just that, a phase. You need both the good and the bad to have balance. You will have days where you are very productive and other days where you feel you haven't been. It may feel that you are constantly fighting against the tide, and no matter how hard you fight, you don't get anywhere. You can either sink and drown or accept that life is full of ebbs and flows and ride it out. Sometimes no matter how hard you try, you cannot fix everything. The fight only encourages more fighting. The struggle and trying harder than ever will kill your chances for success. Sometimes people get so locked onto an idea, a particular route, of determined effort that it becomes part of the problem. Let go, accept this Law, and you will see your salvation through this acceptance. You will see that *"trying harder"* is not the solution. You will see that *"more of the same"* will create *"more of the same"*. Accept the highs and the lows, and you will find balance in your life.

"If you do what you've always done, you'll get what you've always gotten."

Anthony Robbins (1960 -)

American Author, Life Coach, Speaker, and Philanthropist

The Law of Polarity

"Everything is Dual;

- *everything has poles;*

- *everything has its pair of opposites;*

- *like and unlike are the same;*

- *opposites are identical in Nature, but different in degree;*

- *extremes meet;*

- *all truths are but half-truths;*

- *all paradoxes can be reconciled"*

The Kybalion

A Study of the Hermetic Philosophy

This Law means that everything has two *"poles"*, and the Universe is in perfect balance. There is good/bad, love/hate, attraction/disconnection, North/South, masculine/feminine, positive/negative, and fertile/sterile.

Therefore, each of us has good and bad within us. We cannot be all good, and we cannot be all bad; we are a bit of both, and the bit in the middle is balance. When we accept this and find the balance, we are less likely to swing from one side to the other.

So many people try and live a one-sided life. They want the

"good" life and never the bad or negative moments. This way of thinking is unattainable and unsustainable and can make them very unhappy. It is like trying to live life, but with half a person, it is simply not possible. When experiencing the bad, we need to hold ourselves with love, which will help us find balance and acceptance.

The Law of Cause and Effect

"Every Cause has its Effect;

- *every Effect has its Cause;*

- *everything happens according to Law;*

- *Chance is but a name for Law not recognised;*

- there are many planes of causation, but nothing escapes the Law"

The Kybalion

A Study of the Hermetic Philosophy

I first learnt about this Law by listening to Oprah Winfrey.

"Third Law of motion…every action has an equal and opposite reaction…It doesn't matter what you do unto others, it's already been done to you."

Oprah Winfrey (1954 -)

American Talk Show Host, Actress, and Entrepreneur

I rejected it outright. Why? I experienced domestic abuse, coercive control, and financial and psychological abuse for four years. I did nothing in that time apart from loving my former partner, always putting him first, and thinking about his every need. I lived in fear and on eggshells, and I was trauma bonded. I couldn't wrap my head around the words she had spoken. I didn't deserve the abuse.

Every effect has a cause, and every cause has an effect. What does this mean exactly? There can be a chain of causes and effects, so there may not be just one cause. However, a series of actions can all stem from one root cause.

Let us look at weight as an example. My weight has always been a yo-yo, and I still struggle with this. When I have emotions I find challenging to work through, I overeat and end up feeling very sick. The feeling of sickness then masks the feelings I find difficult to process. The triggers are anxiety-based, which links into my subconscious mind, as this is where my habits and behaviours are formed.

Another example is someone who is overweight because they eat the wrong foods and do little or no exercise. The cause is overeating and lack of exercise, and the effect is being an unhealthy weight. However, going on a diet is not enough; you need to look deeper and intend to change this behaviour. No diet will ever *"fix"* this behaviour. You will need to explore why you are triggered into behaving this way. Is it low self-esteem, stress, anxiety, boredom, or lack of sleep? You can change the effect when you have discovered the root cause.

Journalling and meditation have helped me delve deeper and figure out things. Now that I have looked at different areas of my life from an objective perspective, I can see the links. Everything started unfolding like a spider's web, with my paradigm at the centre. I started asking myself what my intention was before I acted on something. Where was that feeling coming from? What would I receive in return? What would I attract back? When you start working from a place of love and not fear, miracles start happening, and we rewrite the paradigm.

I ended up in domestic abuse because of my paradigm, which made me vulnerable to abusive men and relationships. I had low self-esteem and no confidence, and thought controlling, possessive behaviour was normal. I didn't know what personal boundaries were, and I couldn't say "no" to people (not just in relationships but work environments as well); I thought everyone else's needs *had* to come before mine; otherwise, I was selfish and the list goes on. This was the root cause, and the effect was years of domestic abuse. It was a hard pill to swallow, and I struggled to accept it. I went through a phase of beating myself up about it (I still do sometimes). I blamed myself. I hated myself. Then I found the true meaning of forgiveness, self-love and care, and education, and my life changed in ways I didn't think possible.

The Law of Gender

"Gender is in everything;

• everything has its Masculine and Feminine Principles;

• gender manifests on all planes"

The Kybalion

A Study of the Hermetic Philosophy

We all have masculine and feminine principles within us. It is Law. It is sadly very apparent in society today that people reject the masculine or feminine energy within themselves. People wake up unhappy with who they are, and I believe this is because they do not embrace both energies. If a man were told he had intense feminine energy or a female strong masculine energy, they would probably take this as an insult because they do not understand the Law of Gender. There was a time I would have been insulted too! Now I know I need to learn how to balance these energies, and today I took a step in the right direction. My mind, my masculine, looked upon my heart, my feminine. My heart, my feminine, felt my mind, my masculine.

When people are unbalanced, it can lead to miserable lives. In the past, people have been so restricted in their gender roles that they have not felt free to embrace their counterpart energy. Governments and businesses are structured to create a masculine-dominant society for people of all genders. There is not one country on this planet where females have equal rights to males. The word "gender" carries a heavy weight now. The feminine has been suppressed for many generations.

Even though this Law uses the word "gender", it is not referring to sex organs. The Law of Gender refers to masculine and feminine opposing energies types, and for this world to thrive, it needs both in equal amounts. For things to manifest into being and feel fulfillment, we must pull both energies equally. We require to draw energy from both sides in any given situation.

So what does any of this mean?

The Feminine

The Feminine energy represents femininity, Motherhood, pregnancy, and all this could imply. If you are a Father, the feminine is about communication with your children and showing them your nurturing side. The feminine is about embracing your softer side, exploring your emotions and listening to your intuition.

The Feminine symbolises Venus, the planet and Goddess of love, sex and pleasure, and the Moon. The Feminine is growth and expansion and a time of harvest and abundance. This energy is powerful, sensual, kind, caring, gentle, empathic, spiritual, romantic, the creative principle in action, and represents deep beauty in all of its forms. The Feminine is self-care and love for one's self.

The Masculine

The Masculine balances the Feminine's creativity with rules and foundations. The Masculine gives form and shape to the Feminine's expansive Nature. The Masculine can be represented by the Zodiac sign Aries, the Sun and is ruler over the material World. The Masculine is order, structure, and routine, where habits are formed, firmness, strength, assertiveness, formality, discipline, authority and stability. The Masculine sets limits and enforces rules. The Masculine is the dominance of logic over emotion and the mind over the heart.

When we tap into both energies, we can achieve anything. A business with endless new ideas and the discipline to carry them through and be a financial success. A woman who can teach kindness and love but also the ability to say "no" and hold her authority. A man who can give sound logical advice but can communicate with love and empathy. A loving, nurturing Mother who is also a successful businesswoman, a Father who is a successful businessman, and a caring, loving Father. The possibilities are endless.

Chapter Three

Your Environments

There are different ways to strengthen our inner World. In this chapter, we will use intention and some magical tools, for example, the Laws of the Universe, affirmations, meditations, and some energy work.

Your Environments

We have just learnt that our emotions and thought patterns have unlimited power in creating our reality. So let's take a look at what is going on inside you. Are you working from a place of fear or love? In your Journal complete the following activity.

Internal Environment

Internal Environment Exercise

Let's take a look at the things we fear. When we confront our fears, it brings the death of that fear.

On a piece of paper, I want you to write all of your current limiting beliefs around your:

Health and body,

Personal desires and happiness,

Relationships (family, friends and acquaintances),

Career, work and success (even if you are currently unemployed, if you are a full-time parent, this still classifies as full-time work)

Money

Material things and property

An example of money; is money is hard to earn, or you must work hard to make money.

In your Journal, I want you to write about your dream life based on your:

Health and body,

Personal desires and happiness,

Relationships (family, friends and acquaintances),

Career and work (even if you are currently unemployed, if you are a full-time parent, this still classifies as full-time work)

Money

Material things and property

An example of money; I am a money magnet, and money comes to me easily and frequently

Take a look at the difference! Take a look at what you are attracting right now into your life based on your limiting beliefs and fears, and take a look at what you could be attracting into your life. I want you to rip up, cut, or burn (safely) your limiting beliefs. They do not serve you. From now on, I want you to read about your dream life every day. Take a few moments each day to remind yourself of what is possible, and stop thinking about the fear. Stop playing the "worse case scenario" games, and start playing the "Magic" game.

How do we play this excellent Magic game? We play using our feelings. It would be impossible to monitor every thought we have, and we have more than six thousand thoughts daily. We need to feel our way through the day. We can feel good through the positive emotions of gratitude, forgiveness, desire, faith, love, sex, romance, enthusiasm, courage and hope. The negative emotions are anxiety, depression, fear, jealousy, hatred, greed, revenge, superstition and anger. Think about it logically, if you could ask for something, would you ask for something that makes you feel good or bad? You are not going to ask for things that make you feel bad, are you? You are going to want the good stuff!

Positive and negative emotions cannot occupy our minds simultaneously; it is one or the other. When you change your attitude toward situations, people or results, you tap into your imagination, intuition, and perception gifts. These gifts allow us to think from the inside out, which is how the Law of Attraction works.

External Environment

How do we stay positive if our environment is negative and we can't just leave? We may live in a complicated situation where there are external forces we cannot control, for example: a teenager whose parents have mental health problems and abuse alcohol and substances, a broken marriage, redundancy, court, illness, grief, bullying etc. In my case, it was Domestic Abuse.

Whatever you are experiencing now is not going to last forever. You must keep reminding yourself there is a light at the end of the tunnel. Sometimes this light is a flicker because it is far away. Sometimes the light is big and bright because you are coming to the end of this phase. It's OK if you cannot run towards the light, and you need to take it as a crawling walk. Just take one step at a time and in the right direction. It took me two months to leave the abusive relationship and ten months to sell my home, as my former partner was incredibly obstructive. I felt like it was *never* going to end, but I kept reminding myself that everything has an ending. Nothing lasts forever. So when times are tough, the only thing you can do is get tougher.

"Tough times never last, but tough people do."

Dr Robert Schuller (1926 – 2015)

American Christian Televangelist, Pastor, Motivational Speaker, and Author

Finding other people whose light shines brightly will help you through the darkness and the chaos. Find people who inspire you to keep going, and they will help keep you on the right track. Everyone has a story to tell, and you can listen to this in an audio version, books, videos, blogs, and the list goes on. My inspirations are Bob Proctor, Bessel Van Der Kolk, Price Pritchett, Rhonda Byrne, Joseph Murphy, Caroline Sanderson, Jax Robinson, Berenice Tan, Lisa Nichols, Napoleon Hill, and Matthias J Barker. Whoever it is, study them, their work, and how they overcame difficult situations.

It is important to remember that when you feel like a victim or trapped and have no choice, you *still* have a choice. How we respond to our emotions and how we respond to our environment is our freedom alone. Journalling helps you can see the situation clearly. When we have everything whirling around in our heads, it can feel *"big"* and overwhelming. You can see everything from a different perspective when you write things out on paper. I found this so helpful as I felt I had no one to talk to at the time. Journalling, for me, was like talking to a best friend.

Outcome Exercise

Please write down your thoughts exactly as they are. You don't need to defend them, justify them or explain them. Then in a different colour, write down the breakdown, for example: is your weight a problem (do you overeat, eat the wrong items etc.), is the problem your health (have you gone to the G.P.?), are you in debt (are you overspending, do you know where your money goes etc.), is your relationship falling apart (have you seen a marriage counsellor, have you spoken about how you feel, when was the last time you had a date night?).

In another colour, please write down the desired outcome of each situation and how you will achieve it. It's essential to be realistic about the outcome and how it will happen. Time frames are less important, but it is helpful to write some dates. Remember the Natural Laws of the Universe when doing this section, and be honest with yourself. It is not the destination that matters but the journey.

Remember The Law of Polarity, we all have dips in life, but we also experience highs. This links in with the Law of Rhythm, the backwards and forwards motion, good day to bad day, bad day to good day, I'm sure you get the idea. When riding down on the low, it matters how we ride down. Do we ride down to the bottom in fear (which is a matter of perspective), or do we plan for the high on the way down? I prepared for the highs on my way down. Let me explain.

After I had broken up with my former partner and was still living with him, I felt utterly trapped. I could feel fear gripping my heart. I remember listening obsessively too the song *"The Walls Are Way Too Thin"* by Holly Humberstone, thinking that they could have been the thickness of castle walls and still been too thin. Now I could have fallen into utter despair, and I could have become depressed, I could have felt helpless, I could have felt like there was no escape, and I could have done many things. The fear was ready to consume me. What did I do on this journey downward? I planned for the up. I found my faith again. I sat with my Tarot Decks, listened to their guidance, started writing down my plans for the future, and wrote down new business ideas and ways to earn an income. I started going on TikTok and building up an audience. When everything seemed to be working against me when I was trapped inside a house, I could not sell, when I started to regain lost memories, when I started realising the trauma I had been through, I did not crumble. I pulled up my "big girl knickers" (Bridget Jones style!), put on my War Paint (as my best friend Natalie would say!), and stepped out of my comfort zone.

I was still terrified of the person with whom I was living with, and they were not at all pleased I was putting on make-up and looking nice for people on TikTok. He was royally pissed off, and I worried he would burst in whenever I tried recording something. I think the only saving grace was he was fearful I would publish him losing his shit at me. I only started going on TikTok because it was *everywhere* I looked, and I took it as a sign from the Universe. TikTok saved me in some way. I had so many beautiful comments, and everyone was so lovely. It was a *huge* confidence builder and gave me the courage to keep going. TikTok helped me to step into my power and find myself again, and it reconnected me with a world I had been isolated from for years. I freed myself internally, and then on the sixth of December, my Mum turned up with a suitcase out of the blue and told me I was going home with her. Unwittingly I had used my faith and the Law of Attraction to make my dreams of freedom come true.

"To believe in the things you can see and touch is no belief at all; but to believe in the unseen is a triumph and a blessing."

Abraham Lincoln (1809 – 1865)
16th president of the United States

The final step, which links into the next area, is to find someone you have access to, a close friend, a new friend, a new associate, someone in the community, etc., to whom you can share your journey. This is how we keep ourselves accountable for our new goals and our dreams. My person was the beautiful Michaela Chapman, who had also fled domestic abuse. One day, I met her by chance on a walk, and it was like the Universe had lined it all up for us both. We both needed each other, and in an instant, we found each other. Michaela was ten steps ahead of me when it came to court, Police etc., and she shared her experiences and knowledge from a place of love. I would be in a different place today if it weren't for her. Find someone who is running with you or slightly faster than you so you are supported on your journey. Don't find someone you have to drag, but someone running in the same direction. Using these steps, I have now stepped into a new space of possibility and a new level of discomfort as I stretch and move outside my comfort zones.

The Five People Who Surround You

"You're the average of the five people spend the most time with."

Jim Rohn (1930 – 2009)
American Entrepreneur, Author and Motivational speaker

When you start changing your life, you will notice the people in your life will change too. Sometimes our closest friends end up in a different place than us, and we drift apart. But, if it is meant to be, they will return. I have found this on several occasions when I am in a very different place from others. At first, I had trouble accepting this, but then I realised that if I wanted to change my future, the people around me needed to change too.

You can be anything you want and achieve anything as long as you take the required actions. People may start to judge you when you step into your power. It doesn't matter. Their judgement comes from a low frequency, and it is essential not to let this lower your frequency. Do not meet their negativity with negativity, as you will only attract more. Meet their negativity with love. They are acting out this way because their perspective is limited, and they haven't mastered their minds. You cannot control what is going on in the World, and you cannot control what someone else thinks. The only control you have is what is going on inside your mind, which is all that matters. The more you can control your mind and emotions, the more empowered you will feel.

It is no surprise when I say you will encounter people who are just difficult in every way. Their mind is distorted, they are cynical, everything is doom and gloom, and they are generally sour about life. This could be because of experiences in the past, or they have attracted the wrong sort of people into their lives. As I said above, do not return the energy in the form of dislike, but hold compassion and understanding in your heart. They will try and turn you, as misery loves company, but when you recognise that creative intelligence within you, you will remain calm, unmoved and un-triggered. You will see that sending them healing, empathy, and compassion will change them positively and beautifully. Miracles can happen if you speak, act and think in true accordance with the Principle of Harmony.

What can we do if the person tries to force their will or viewpoint on us by having a temper tantrum, using emotional blackmail, crying or other forms of manipulation? Do not permit them to try and take advantage of you. I know this is easier said than done, and sometimes even now, I slip up still. It is best if you remain firm but kind and refuse to yield. An example of this could be your boss wanting you to work on days you are not available or to work overtime. It could be anyone, but remember, appeasement never wins. Another person cannot annoy or upset you unless you allow them to. You have a choice to be emotionally mature and have the freedom to have understanding, goodwill and respect for them.

Chapter Four

Soul Work

We Are All Made of Star Dust

In the 1980s, a theory came to light in a thirteen-part television series called "Cosmos" aired on PBS. It was hosted by an astronomer named Carl Sagan, who spoke about science and history-related topics on the Earth, its evolution, life's origin, and the solar system.

"We are a way for the Universe to know itself. Some part of our being knows this is where we came from. We long to return. And we can, because the cosmos is also within us. We're made of star stuff."

Carl Sagan (1934 – 1996)

American astronomer

Humans, animals and other forms of life are created of carbon, nitrogen, and oxygen atoms and atoms of all other heavy elements. These elements were first created in starts over four and a half billion years ago. Therefore we are literally made of Star Dust, or Star Stuff, as Chris Impey, professor of astronomy at the University of Arizona, would put it.

The knowledge that we are created out of the same materials as the beautiful stars themselves, made in the image of God/Divine/Spirit/Universe, and all connected is an inspiration in itself. Moreover, we can tap into this infinite energy through various points in our bodies called Chakras.

Aura and Luminous Body

To fully understand your Chakras, you need a basic understanding of your Aura. The Aura is an egg-shaped fluid and fluctuating energy surrounding your physical body. There are seven layers to the Auric field: the Etheric Body, Astral or Emotional Body, Lower Mental Body, Higher Mental Body, Spiritual Body, Causal Body and Ketheric Body. It is not necessary for you to learn all the meanings of these. These energy fields all coexist together and can be measured on sensitive instruments. In 1908 Dr Walter Kilner developed a camera that could capture the Aura on film. The Aura acts as a platform for informational energy to back and forth from our bodies to the Universe.

Aura Exercise

Sit in a darkened room with your hands in front of you. Rub them vigorously together and hold them slightly apart with your finger curved slightly, as if you were holding a ball, gaze softly past your fingertips. Against the darkened background, you should see very fine lines of light, or a colourless light, moving between your fingertips.

Sometimes you can see people's Auric field if they are sat against a particular colour wall, usually a light blue. You will see a misty, hazy light around their head.

To feel the Aura sit in a relaxed position, take three deep breaths and hold your hands in front of you. Start with them held shoulder distance apart, and fingers cupped, again as if you were holding a ball, and start moving them slowly towards each other. You will get to a point where your hands may start to feel warm, and then you will feel resistance as if there was a ball of energy in your hands. This is your Aura!

Chakra System

You might have heard of the term Chakras used in yoga or other practices and wondered what they do. All over the World, it is believed that there is a life force that can be used in spiritual traditions and healing systems. This life force has many names but is commonly known as our Auric Energy Field.

The chakras are energy points in the body that are linked to our physical organs. Seven major chakras and twenty-two interconnected smaller ones are located at different points around the body. Our Chakras connect us to a broader cosmic field called the Quantum Field.

When the chakras are balanced, they are associated with a

colour and elements, which some people can see, or sense. However, sometimes these energy points can become blocked when energy is not flowing correctly. Healers can help shift these blockages and balance them, but you can also do this yourself using meditation, visualisation and colour breathing exercises. I recommend Patricia Mercier, bestselling author of *"The Chakra Bible"* and her book called *"The Chakra Experience"* if you want to learn about them in much more depth.

Here is a very brief description of the main Chakras:

Crown

- **Associated colour:** Violet, white or gold light.

- **Element:** Thought.

- **Location:** This is located at the top of your head.

- **How it links to our physical bodies:** The pineal gland needs light to function. It releases melatonin which helps us regulate sleep and when it is time to wake up.

- **Illnesses:** Emotional withdrawal after trauma and finding life difficult, psychological disorders.

This chakra helps us connect with the Universe. It helps us to receive messages and ideas. The Crown helps with spiritual awareness and is open during meditation.

Third Eye

- **Associated colour:** Indigo.

- **Element:** Light.

- **Location:** This is located just above your eyes on your forehead.

- **How it links to our physical bodies:** Nervous system, sinuses, and Pituitary gland. This master gland regulates other glands, for example, the thyroid and adrenals. It also regulates growth and our reproductive hormones.

- **Illnesses:** sinusitis, nervous disorders, hormone imbalance, migraines.

This chakra is linked to psychic powers, higher intuition, and keeping an open mind, and it provides us with insight.

Throat

- **Associated colour:** Blue.

- **Element:** Sound.

- **Location:** This is located at your throat.

- **How it links to our physical bodies:** nervous system, jaw, parathyroid gland and Thyroid gland. This gland regulates metabolism by using iodine. Too much or too little iodine causes excess body weight or loss.

- **Illnesses:** Problems with the throat, and respiratory system, tension problems in the neck and shoulder area.

This chakra is linked with speaking the truth, self-expression, and listening to intuition.

Heart

- **Associated colour:** Green.

- **Element:** Air.

- **Location:** This is located at your heart (the name says it all).

- **How it links to our physical bodies:** heart, circulation, lungs, immune system, and thymus gland. This gland plays a big part in the functioning of major organs. It regulates the lymphatic system, which in turn immune system.

- **Illnesses:** AIDS, heart attacks, substance abuse.

  The heart chakra is connected with our love for ourselves and others and teaches forgiveness, empowerment, compassion and happiness.

Solar Plexus

- **Associated colour:** Yellow.

- **Element:** Fire.

- **Location:** This is located around your upper abdomen and your gut.

- **How it links to our physical bodies:** adrenal glands, stomach, digestive system, liver and pancreas. This organ produces insulin to either store or uses the sugar needed by the cells. It is also stimulated by the duodenum to produce digestive juices.

- **Illnesses:** ulcers, bowel disorders, anxiety, arthritis.

  This chakra is associated with the subconscious, self-worth, the centre of personal power, and freedom.

Sacral

- **Associated colour:** Orange.

- **Element:** Water.

- **Location:** This is located in your lower abdomen and sexual organs.

- How it links to our physical bodies: digestive system, hormones, reproductive system and adrenals glands. These glands not only secrete sex hormones but are also stimulated by different emotions to produce adrenaline.

- **Illnesses:** reproductive problems, STD, AIDS, bowel and bladder problems.

This chakra can motivate us to grow and change. It can help support emotional pleasure and self-respect.

Base/Root

- **Associated colour:** Red.

- **Element:** Earth.

- **Location:** This is at the base of your body and points downwards.

- **How it links to our physical bodies:** spine, bladder, kidneys, nervous system, adrenal glands and parathyroid gland. This set of four glands regulates how much calcium is in the blood, which contributes to healthy bones and nerves.

- **Gonads:** Women – ovaries: Controls our feminine physiological characteristics and emotions.

- **Men – testes:** Controls our masculine physiological characteristics and emotions

- **Illnesses:** Hip and leg problems.

It is our grounding chakra and links us to the Earth, our physical body, and the World.

There are countless online meditations you can find to use on your Chakras, and I recommend finding one you like and bringing it into your meditation routine.

Chakra Drawing Exercise

Let us develop your intuition by sensing and drawing your chakra energies. There is no right or wrong for this. In your Journal, sketch out an outline of a person, draw a stick man, or list the Chakras and the colours beside them. You will use a selection of coloured pencils to colour in your person.

Firstly sit quietly for a moment, still your mind and release any emotions that surface. Forget all you know about Chakras and their colours. I want you to sense your unique energies. You can work from your Crown Chakra down or your Base Chakra up; it doesn't matter.

When you are ready, draw your colours without thinking. Use your intuition and follow that gut feeling. Remember, there is no right or wrong.

Let us look at the results, and remember this is an exercise to tune into your intuition:

Red: strength, courage, passion, desire, sexual energy.

Excessive Red: Misplaced sexual energy, violence, anger.

Orange: change, energetic, creativity.

Excessive Orange: imbalance, attention seeking.

Yellow: happiness, joy, change.

Excessive Yellow: deceit, cowardice, grief, mourning.

Pink: unconditional love.

Excessive Pink: ungrounded.

Green: abundance, growth, grounded, balanced.

Excessive Green: envy, jealousy, unwillingness

Turquoise Blue/Blue: peace, guidance, spiritual or religious guidance, strong, reliable.

Excessive Turquoise Blue/Blue: sadness, grief, loss.

Violet and Purple: spiritual development, wealth, abundance, creativity, imagination.

Excessive Violet and Purple: ungrounded person, excessiveness, stagnant.

Brown: grounded, power, strength, traditional,

wholesomeness, dependability, reliability, steadfastness.

Excessive Brown: depression, repressed anger, negativity, unbalanced, dominance, dull, unyielding, stubborn.

Small amounts of Black: grounded, power, elegance, formality, mystery, traditional or unconventional.

Excessive Black: mourning, depression, repressed anger, negativity, unbalanced, addictions, dominance.

Grey: Authority, control, formality, conservative.

Excessive Grey: repression, un-wellness, moody, depression, cool.

Look at the outcome of the exercise, and in your, Journal answer these questions:

How did this exercise affect me?

What have I learnt from it?

What changes can I make?

Meditation Is Key

Why is meditation so important? Meditation can help relax the body, promote healing, aid memory, help come up with original ideas, change your perspective, change your mindset and connect us to the Universe. Meditation is Magical and can help transform our lives. Meditation helps keep the mind healthy, uncluttered and working to the best of its ability.

Concerning our health, meditation can:

- release muscular tension;

- lower high blood pressure;

- stimulates the immune system and produces white blood cells;

- opens constricted air passages;

- increases blood circulation to the digestive system, skin and brain;

- dramatically effects hormonal activity;

- balances the right and left hemisphere and can help with insomnia, chronic pain, hypertension and speeds up recovery after illness.

I was very reluctant to start meditating every day. I thought I never had a chance to wee, let alone meditate! My life has been a hamster wheel for as long as I can remember. I had to commute long distances to get to my secondary school, and I had to study constantly because I am, in fact, severely dyslexic (writing this book was a miracle in itself!). I helped run the family business and helped my parents decorate and renovate houses in between studies, and then I went to university and worked three jobs. I left university and worked two jobs totalling up to eighty hours a week sometimes. Days off were a *dream*! I then ended up experiencing four years of domestic abuse and coercive control, so not exactly a time to meditate. Now I am a full-time single Mum who also works. When on earth would I find time to sit listening to calm music, light candles, fan some incense and meditate? I am sure many of you can relate to this. So how did I do it?

Many of us function in a memory state which is a state of mind that is on autopilot. We operate from old paradigms, behavioural patterns and thought patterns from our subconscious mind. Remember what I said in the First Chapter? The paradigm is formed from our childhood experiences, and unless we were fortunate, it is generally formed around scarcity, lack and fear-based limiting beliefs. To meditate is your highest honour. So why don't more of us do it? People don't meditate because they won't find time for it. To meditate is self-love and self-care. The state of our mind is not at the top of our priority list. It wasn't on mine! I felt I wasn't worthy of having *"me time"*. Who was I to put myself first? If people went to the doctors for mental health problems, and the doctor offered pills or meditation, which one would most people choose? The paradigm needs to change to create new behaviour. You need to change the paradigm, or the new meditation habit won't stick, and you will give up after a few days or weeks.

Think of your phone as an example. You plug it into recharge when the battery is low so that you can use it effectively. Likewise, think of meditation as a charger for your mind. You must meditate for your mind to work to the best of its ability. We need to connect to the Universe, which gives us more energy, grounds us, and shifts our state of mind, so we are more aware of the miracles happening around us.

Meditation is not sitting cross-legged on the floor, burning candles and incense, whilst humming and chanting. I thought it was! But I was very wrong! Many forms of meditation vary from having a still body to moving through various positions with a mindful and slow pace. There is also visualisation, mantra and affirmations, sensing objects and breath and body awareness. Guided Breathwork is a form of meditation that works wonders for me. Berenice Tan, a Breathwork Teacher Trainer, has some beautiful Breathwork meditations, and I highly recommend her. The only way to find out which is best for you is by trying them out.

I cannot commit to meditating every day. Having a hyperactive toddler who potentially has Autism doesn't permit it. I meditate four times a week, and I am happy with this for now. It is better to meditate three to five times a week and be consistent than meditate every day for two weeks and then give up. You may go through periods of meditation and then stop for a while, but once you have seen the Magic that can come from meditation, then you will go back to it. The aim is to meditate every day, but you need to start from somewhere, and being proud of what you can accomplish is very important. As you create a new habit, hold yourself with love, and the habit will be easier to form.

Beginning Your Journey

Meditation is a personal journey and is not a case of one style fits all. Experiment with different types at various times. When you first start, aim for ten minutes and then you can build your way up. It's going to feel different at first, but then you will see that answers will come to you much more quickly, little miracles will start happening, you will be more in tune, and the World will start looking a little different.

It is easier to stick to the meditations if you do them consistently at the same time every day. I am a creature of habit, like many of us are. Try meditations first thing in the morning, before you go to bed at night, or both! Spot meditations (see below) are very powerful too, and they can give you that little boost here and there.

When you first start meditating, you will notice a change in your brain between the alpha and beta states. You may also feel sore in different areas of your body as you learn to scan your body. Don't worry, though, because it will feel better after the mediation. We become more self-aware when we relax and let go of trivial thoughts. This self-awareness releases fear, anxiety, tension and stress. You do not have to do anything, just acknowledging it releases it. As soon as you notice it, the pressure releases automatically. Self-awareness brings inner peace and harmony. It doesn't matter how chaotic our lives are, when we relax, we find tranquility and enjoy the smaller moments. Even our concentration starts to strengthen, and we can focus on something to the best of our ability without having countless trivial thoughts. Problem-solving becomes more accessible as the mind filters out irrelevant distractions, and we witness things from a bird's eye point of view, giving a sense of clarity. And in a flash, you will be able to see things for what they are.

Spot Meditation Exercise

An example of a spot meditation is a red traffic light. I used to become annoyed every time I hit a red traffic light. I was always in a rush! But now, when I approach a red traffic light, I think I have a whole two minutes to do nothing, and I smile.

In those two minutes, you can:

breathe in deeply, hold, and breathe out

let your mind and body relax and slow down

soften your face, especially around your jaw, and soften your stomach

become aware of any tension in your body

have two whole minutes to breathe and relax

As the light turns green, you can focus on your task at hand, which is driving safely and well. And look forward to the next red light!

The Power of a Pen – Journalling

Journalling has endless benefits, and I will cover some in this section. I have always journaled, and I believe I have never suffered from depression because of this. At one time, I did have symptoms of Post Traumatic Stress Disorder, but I managed to escape this narrowly. I have no evidence that it was the journalling, but I believe it to be true. Journalling is recommended in many therapies and is a powerful healing tool.

Some of the exercises in this book have gone in your Journal already, but I want you to try and get in the habit of writing in your Journal. As I mentioned before, I have severe dyslexia, and writing is not a hobby of mine! However, as a child, I always felt compelled to write in a journal or diary. *"Back in the day"*, I had to use a dictionary whenever I wrote in my Journal, but now I ask Siri if I need help, so there is no excuse!

Like meditation, journalling helps you to relax and become more self-aware. Becoming self-aware can be an uncomfortable experience, but it is necessary for growth. We tend to live in our heads, but journalling can bring us down to earth and evoke mindfulness. We experience relief from strong repressed emotions through grounding ourselves, which helps the brain regulate emotions. When we feel better, we have greater confidence and self-identity.

Mental Health

When you journal, you remain in the present as you write, which helps you keep your perspective on everyday life. The feeling of pen on paper is one of life's small pleasures, and it can help you manage anxiety and cope with depression and other mental illnesses. Writing down your thoughts on paper is a release, and you feel lighter afterwards. Also, you can see your problems in front of you, which will help you gain a deeper understanding of your inner deeper conflicts while exploring your external ones. You will start to see that your fears, problems and concerns will surface, and you can address them with a different perspective. The solutions to your problems will appear in front of you on paper, as if by Magic.

Self Confidence

When you start feeling better, and when you can start managing your anxiety levels, you begin to *glow*! This is because your whole frequency changes to a higher one, and your energy field is brighter. Think about the colours in your

Aura changing.

You will feel more prepared to deal with problems. Solutions will come more quickly, and your thoughts will be more organised. You will be making time to care for yourself and prioritise your needs. You will feel in control as you can see yourself ticking off those tasks on your to-do lists that you haven't completed yet.

As you journal in a positive self-talk way, you will start valuing yourself more and building on healthy boundaries with others, and all of your relationships will improve.

Emotional Intelligence

I always thought I was emotionally intelligent, but when I started journalling, it took it to a whole different level. I didn't fully understand emotional intelligence, and I thought it was about being in touch with your feelings. But it is so much more.

Journalling can help you to make sense of what you are feeling. You can tap into why a person, situation, or problem makes you feel a certain way. You start to pick up what your triggers are and why. Writing down honestly what you feel is a discovery of yourself. Make sure there is no judgement when you journal, and hold yourself with love. Remember the Laws of the Universe? We all have good and bad sides to us, and it's about finding the balance. When we get to know ourselves better, we develop a deeper understanding of our reactions, strengths, and weaknesses, as well as what environments help us to thrive!

You will also get to a point where people, situations or circumstances won't irritate, annoy or disappoint you unless you allow them to. The only way another person or situation can upset or annoy you is through your own thoughts. When we are upset or angry, we move through four stages; thoughts, emotions, reactions and actions. Emotional maturity means you can rise above the lower negative frequencies and act on higher frequencies, for example, peace, love, calmness, and tranquillity.

Goals

We *all* need goals. Goals give us a purpose and something to help us to work towards, and they also send the intention of your plans out to the Universe. When we accomplish those goals, we create a sense of achievement, which makes us feel excellent! These positive, high vibrations then attract more abundance into our lives. When you set a goal, you start taking steps to monitor your progress and are motivated to achieve it.

I'm sure most of you have heard of SMART goals; Specific, Measurable, Achievable, Relevant, and Time-bound. If you look up SMART goals, there are many explanations for them, but they generally speak for themselves. You can use your Journal to make SMART goals in any area of your life, start working towards achieving them and troubleshoot any challenges that arise. Write a goal on a piece of card and carry it with you. Read it often throughout the day. I have attached mine to my phone, so I read it every time I look at it.

Creativity

If you are creative, you probably have several ideas buzzing around your head all at once. Journalling allows you to express these ideas and make a log of them so none are forgotten. A journal is a great place to jot them down quickly, and you can revise the ideas later. Even if you don't consider yourself creative, you will still have ideas to write down and develop. You don't need to write down your ideas, but you can draw them or scrapbook them.

Memory

When we write down something, we use the muscles in our hands. The act of using muscles while thinking improves memory. Some schools now have their maths classes in the gym hall. Teachers get the children to run while doing mathematical games, which has dramatically increased how much information is remembered and understood.

When you write, you are committing ideas to memory in a very effective way. Writing is also very therapeutic. In practical terms, you can also refer to anything you have written in your Journal. For example, I used mine as evidence for the Police when I had to report a former partner of Domestic Abuse. When I suffered memory loss around my traumas, I could re-read the events and work through repressed emotions.

Critical Thinking and Communication

Reflective journalling has been proven in many published articles to improve critical thinking, and it can heighten academic performance. Critical thinking is an intellectually disciplined process where we can process and evaluate information that has been observed, reasoned, communicated or experienced. This skill is valuable in everyday situations, business, work or learning environments. Of course, writing every day or several times a week will naturally improve our written skills and the way we communicate both verbally and in writing, enhancing our academic performance. Now you might think you left school a while ago, and this skill is not needed, but you might go back to studying at some point or need this skill within a work environment. Learning never stops, and it shouldn't.

Physical Health

Now, you might be thinking, how on earth does writing help our physical health? Apart from working our hand muscles, what other muscles does it work?

Healthily expressing ourselves can improve liver function, reduce blood pressure, and improve our immune system and overall physical health. It is not the act of writing but the act and power of relaxing. When we are relaxed, our stress hormones and adrenalin levels decrease. This is the Magic of journalling and its healing powers. When we relax, healing takes place.

TIP

Every night in your Journal, write down five things you are grateful for. Journalling will help you see where you are in the moment and will raise your frequency before you fall asleep. Feel the emotions of gratefulness, and you will attract more things to be grateful for in your life.

Goals Exercise

How to attract health, healthy relationships, money etc

In your Journal:

Every morning say a positive affirmation to yourself. There are many examples on the World Wide Web, or write your one, for instance: Today is going to be a wonderful day, the world is filled with abundance and opportunities, and they flow towards me easily. *Or,* I am a money magnet, and money flows towards me with abundance and ease. *Or,* Thank you, Universe, for my Divine protection. Thank you, Universe, for my family's Divine protection. We are and will always remain safe, loved and whole. Thank you, thank you, thank you.

Create a list of ten goals (I have nine goals, with the tenth one to make the main one – do what works for you)

Establish a date for these goals – this is very important, and it is OK to use an estimate. Just make sure you write down something.

If you do not know what you want, think about what you do not what. That will tell you what you want!

Write your goals in the present. For example, I am so grateful and thankful now that...

Reflect on your past successes and create new evidence that you can achieve anything

Start responding positively to life and being aware of your thoughts, have faith, hope, love, courage and tolerance.

Before you eat or drink something, thank the Divine. This is very simple but a great way to start practising gratitude. When we are grateful, we attract more things into our life that we are grateful for.

Chapter Five

Mastering your Emotions

Faith

We very briefly touched on prayer and faith previously in the book. Let's take a much closer look.

We have already established it doesn't matter what you believe in: it matters what your subconscious mind believes. Remember, your subconscious mind has the power to make it come true through connecting to the Divine. Your power is making your subconscious *believe* in what you want to be true, which can be done through prayer and faith. When we pray, we imprint it on our subconscious mind, and our subconscious mind then works to make this thought come true. Now you will start to understand that believing in something that can harm you is foolish. It is not the thing you believe in that will harm you, but your thoughts that you can be harmed by it. The belief in your mind and the thoughts will attract the circumstances, events and actions that will harm you.

I genuinely believe in my faith. People have told me that my unyielding solid faith inspires them. I now know the powers of my subconscious mind (I wrote this book against all odds), but I also believe in the Divine and the Universe. Your beliefs are your own, so find out what they are; from there, they will grow and develop.

What is faith? Faith is one of the three most powerful emotions, faith, love and sex. Faith and love are emotional and spiritual and form part of our psychic, and sex is biological and of the body. I will be discussing Sex Magic later in the book. When you mix the emotion of faith with your intellectual mind, you are speaking directly to the Divine (the Infinite Mind) in a harmonious and balanced way.

"If thou canst believe, all things are possible to him that believeth."

MARK 9:23

The Holy Bible, King James Version

How to Develop Faith

My faith has never been this strong before. Over the years, I dipped in and out of prayer, and for a while, I wasn't allowed to practice my faith due to my controlling, abusive partner. Then, using my Tarot Cards strengthened my faith and built on it. I have always been Pagan, but through the practice of prayer, my faith grew and grew. Faith is a state of mind that can be achieved through prayer, casting spells, autosuggestion, or positive affirmations. My faith began to flourish when I first had faith in myself, which is the root of all Faith.

If you have no faith, it is incredibly challenging to describe how to develop faith. It would be like describing colour to a blind person. Prayer would be the first place to start, as prayer imprints onto the subconscious mind. Autosuggestion or positive affirmations are saying the same thing repeatedly, and eventually, your subconscious mind will accept it. It would take longer with no feelings attached, but it is possible when you start seeing the outcome manifesting into your physical reality, you begin to develop faith. This is because there is no evidence that your prayers have worked. When you repeat the process, your faith will start to develop and that necessary emotion and frame of mind. Faith is developed through practice and not just by following instructions. Faith is very personal and intimate.

"Let Go And Let God."

Bob Proctor (1934 – 2022)
Canadian Author and creator of Proctor Gallagher Institute

Faith is about letting go of doubts, limiting beliefs, fears, anxiety, and other low-frequency emotions. It is about *knowing* that everything will be OK, taking a leap of faith and handing over our desires to the Divine. It is about believing in the Universe's Natural Laws, knowing that they are working whether we believe it or not! I started to believe in myself and have faith in myself, but it wasn't always enough. I was so scared about my court cases. I was so afraid of the Police and giving statements against my former partner, and I held so much fear in my heart. My dearest friend Michaela Chapman told me that she *believed* everything would be fine and "*believed in me*". She told me that *"the truth will always come to light"*. I didn't believe it. I couldn't understand how, but *she believed* it, and that's all I needed. I trusted her belief. I started saying her sentence, "*the truth will always come to light,*" over and over and over again. It consumed my thoughts. The feelings of fear slowly dissipated, and hope started taking form. The repetition built the foundation of my belief, and still, to this day, I believe it, even though it wasn't mine, to begin with.

My belief manifested through my prayer, and my desire became my reality. The Court case was still ongoing at the time of writing this book, but I have had the desired outcome so far. The truth did come to light, and the lies were exposed. The opposing party went to great lengths to conceal the truth, but because I prayed and believed, it all came out.

Faith is the ability to believe in the incredible and to see the invisible. If you do as Bob Proctor says, "*Let Go and Let God, "* you believe in the Universe's Natural Laws and that whatever needs to happen for you to achieve your goals will happen. If you sit back and expect it to fall into your lap, you are mistaken. You need to act. Energy is channelled and goes where you intend it to go. The Divine only helps those who help themselves first.

Michaela Chapman

linktr.ee/i.am.michaela

Level 3 Psychology & Counselling Student (due 2023), Tantra Diploma, NLP Diploma, Life Coaching Diploma, Trauma-informed activist with long-term sobriety, dedicated to helping women & children, Domestic abuse advocate

When Kitty asked me to write some words for her book, I was worried about how I'd find the time as things have been overwhelming as a solo parent, and my brain thinks I need the setting and space to be "perfect" to get the clarity to write. Or it tells me not to do it now because it won't be "good enough." This is a life-long thought line I'm aware of. And here I am... Writing regardless and despite all the narration "up there." My toddler is in the room next door. We've just finished dinner. My back is in pain. I have guilt that I should be focused on him. But as with all I've got through and overcame, I know I do good for him by doing good for me.

I'm currently 34. I got clean and sober eight years ago. I'm a missed-ectopic pregnancy survivor – and this was something Kitty and I related to on that beautiful day we met. We were walking separately with our new babies up in a remote village. It was just us. I spoke to her, and we connected divinely. I could write a chapter on our meeting and connection... And so... Here I now am, writing for her book. God, I'm so proud of her.

I'm a survivor of domestic abuse. I'm a solo parent. I got through the pandemic as a newly single Mum, alone in the house. I've gone from living in a women's refuge to owning my own home. And we now have a dog. Throughout the pandemic, I dealt with my Mother's cancer diagnosis, family court and two criminal cases. I litigated myself through court because I hadn't paid enough of my mortgage to be entitled to legal aid, even though domestic abuse was involved.

I've been failed time and time again by systems. And time and time again – I have risen. No matter how tough things got – the phone calls, the emails, the court hearings, the course work, the finances... There was always this golden ball of Faith in truth and love in my deepest, most sacred part. Right in the pit, and the energetic trust, would permeate through. I HAD to believe. I KNEW in the belief. Years of inner work got me to this Divine place.

I'm a seeker. I sought truth everywhere through my battles. I listened to what rang true deep within and not just by the mind to what "sounded good." So I think critically – albeit it can seem a minefield within my mind; with that ability, I trust in the blessing of having it.

I prayed. Meditated. Breathed consciously. Drank water. Ate well. Got sleep. I wrote to my inner kid and love letters to myself. I burnt sage and palo santo. I became friends with the moon and could feel its femininity. I called on her. I called on ancestors and tribes of women gone before me. I asked for help from safe women around me. I rang and emailed for support groups and help. I texted. I shared my resentments and rage. I brewed and sipped on cacao. I ACCEPTED help. And none of this I have done "perfectly."

But I've kept going, whether it be a trudge or in a carried-felt flow.

I gained experience of staying with myself through the trials, enough to build a catalogue of memory to reflect on what I'd overcome. Staying with myself and sitting with all the feelings and hearing them out became more accessible to me when I realised me doing that would be the best example for my child. By helping myself, I help him. We co-regulate together. And today, I KNOW that not only is he a gift to me, and I am to him. And that's a bold statement for this World. To love and teach him adequately and healthily, I had to be full of ME and not the World's messages, warped conditioning and centuries of misogynistic wiring.

Faith in truth and love has been my foundation for everything I have got through. There were periods of real depression, anxiety and the most crippling of triggers that oozed out physically. There are daily judgmental thoughts of myself. Yet right at the core, there is the truth. And so my job and responsibility are to redirect my internal spotlight there repeatedly... To push through the layers and filters of so much the World has piled on my lens and find that wordless place. That God-state. There is where I see and feel my worth. My lovability. My enough-ness. My truth. The One-ness. With this place known to me, I can get through anything. The knowing is not always profound, although it can be. And this is so more than OK. This has been my experience.

I have got three Diploma distinctions in Neuro-Linguistic Programming – Dealing with Depression, Life Coaching and Tantra, and I continue learning. I've done workshops with the British Institute of Human Rights and completed the Freedom Programme and Alpha Vesta course. I gained training in trauma-informed responses and completed the Support through Court course with the Open University. I have also self-taught myself a lot in many areas.

The answer for me is always to go back within. Everything comes down to beliefs. And in my experience, this does not mean you're this perfect, non-fearful, floaty, zen-like person... But a complex human, with traumas, triggers and all sorts of non-perfect-ness, yet knows that wordless place where that core belief resides, where she can retreat to remember the truth. Even in all the mess or the beauty... And keep going. Keep trudging. And Mother-loving.

RISE.

Prayer

Prayer comes in many forms. I learnt how to pray from my Father, and then slowly developed the skill in alignment with my values and beliefs. However, the earliest prayers I can remember were our mealtime ones. Before every meal, we used to pray in German (I am German, Irish and English), and it was a prayer of giving thanks for our food. At the time, I did not understand why we did it, but now I know that being grateful for our food is a simple way of attracting more to be thankful for.

Translation:

"Come Lord Jesus,

Be our guest,

And let these gifts

To us be blest.

Amen" - Anonymous

Remember what we said above? Prayer is *desire*. Pray in times of plenty and not just in times of crisis. We speak to the Divine through our subconscious mind when we pray. When we pray, we enter a frame of mind that allows us to talk to the subconscious, which speaks to the Divine or other Beings you may pray to. People pray to different beings: celestial beings, ascended masters, ancient beings, elemental beings, angels, archangels, animal and plant guides, spirit guardians, the old and the new gods, or directly to the Divine Source.

You can pray anytime, anywhere, active or still. I pray whilst walking down the street, and I say a particular prayer in my mind if I see a particular colour truck or car, I say, "*The court case is finished in Divine Order*", and I say it with a heart full of love. I saw the pain my Mother was going through regarding the court case, and to empower her and fill her heart with love, I taught her the power of prayer. I asked my Mother to do the same as I was doing, and she did. At first, she found it challenging to hold love in her heart as she spoke the words, but after repeating the prayer every time she saw that colour, her spirits lifted, and the fear and pain dissipated. You might be wondering why that colour and why a truck. It was at the time the colour and model of the person's truck taking me to court.

I used to be consumed by fear every time I saw that colour. I actively wanted to change my emotions and frequencies to attract my desires. I knew fear would only attract more fearful situations. I knew I had to stop this if I genuinely wanted protection. Love conquers *all*. I also knew the power of other people's emotions and the power of my Mum's subconscious mind. I explained to her how the Laws of the Universe worked and how forgiveness and love were hundreds of more times powerful than feelings of fear and hate. This simple sentence gave my Mum so much strength and healing.

Positive Affirmations and Auto Suggestions are a form of prayer. When we pay, we tend to repeat the same verse or phrase repeatedly. Prayer can therefore be negative or positive. It is, therefore, important to say your prayers positively. Sending negativity out to the Divine will only attract more negativity towards us. If your prayer is along the lines of "I can't, I'm afraid, I'm scared", etc., you will attract more of this. If you want to pray effectively and ask for guidance to help you negative the problems, the Divine is designed to run, fetch and deliver. "I want…" will not work. There needs to be that element of *trust* that everything will work out. We need to *trust* and *believe* that we will receive guidance, and then we can *act* on the messages and co-create the desired outcome.

"It has been proven now scientifically that an affirmative thought is hundreds of times more powerful than a negative thought."

Michael Bernard Beckwith (1956 -)
Founder and CEO of the Agape International Spiritual Center

Prayer Exercise

We will look at prayer but worded in two different ways. One way is going to be attracting more negativity, and the second version is going to be attracting positive outcomes. I will use the word "God" instead of Universe to keep things simple. After you have compared the two prayers, I want you to write in your Journal some simple positive prayers for areas in your life where you are struggling or are having difficulties.

TIP

When you are writing your prayer, remember that

"What things soever ye desire, when ye pray,

believe that ye receive them,

and ye shall have them."

MARK 11:24

The Holy Bible, King James Version

Example one: attracting more negative situations

Oh God,

If you are listening, please help me. I am in so much dept, and I need money. Living costs have gone up, and I can't afford anything! The bills are mounting up, and I am so scared. I don't know how to make more money, and I don't know where I can get more money from. I am already working myself to death. Oh God, please, please, please help me. I need more money to put food on the table, I don't have enough money. Please God if you are listening to me, I need your help. I don't really pray to you, but I promise to make more effort if you help me. If you are up there listening, please help me. I deserve to live a good life.

Example two: attracting positive outcomes

God,

I am so grateful and thankful for all that I receive. I am thankful I am now attracting wealth and success to my experience. Dear God, I am grateful that money is circulating freely in my life and that I have achieved economic health. I am thankful I am a money magnet and use it wisely and constructively. I release money with joy, and money returns me a thousandfold. I am grateful now that situations, circumstances and events that help me achieve success are flowing towards me. Thank you, thank you, thank you.

See the difference?

If you are coming up blank with writing a prayer, or you feel like you are lying to yourself by saying you are attracting wealth and abundance, you can repeat the words: love, wealth, success, and happiness slowly several times a day. These words are *powerful*, and your subconscious will attract them. Those words are a great symbol of abundance, and your life will start attracting magic. Then, when you feel more comfortable with the idea of having love, wealth, success, and happiness, you can develop them into prayers.

For an effective prayer, you need to acknowledge the problem, turn it over to your subconscious mind to change, and have a deep conviction that it will be done.

The Sixth Sense – Intuition

We are never alone, even when we think we are. We are surrounded by our guides all of the time. Our guides are the beings we choose to spend this life with. They are here cheerleading you every step of the way and are here to make sure you stay on your path. Unfortunately, many of us fall off of this path because we are taught in society to *"be small"* and to *"stay safe"*. As a result, we are not aligned with our true purpose, and we repress our true feelings and emotions. This then gets stored in our bodies, and health problems manifest.

Our intuition grows when we open our hearts and start shifting things that no longer serve us. We listen to our bodies, and our souls sing; we expand and create and manifest our true desires. We develop our intuition, also known as our sixth sense. When we start tapping into messages we receive from our guides and the Divine and acting with the truth, we become genius. We have this inner knowing, and we can navigate our way around any situation. We have foresight on how situations may unfold, we are emotionally intelligent, and our decisions align with our values and truth. We work from a place of love and desire and experience the magic of living in the moment.

When we start listening to the Divine, our guides and our intuition or gut feeling, we start seeing magical manifestations and opportunities flowing into our lives. When we work on high-level frequencies, our awareness expands, and we begin to see the possibilities of the magical life we can create. We also see how Divinely supported we are and how held and loved we are. How can we not be? We are all a unique expression of the Universe experiencing itself.

Speaking to our Guardians Exercise

Create a space where you wish to pray. This can be outside your garden, in a park, or at the seaside. You can create a space in your home which personal or shared by the family, or you can go to a place of worship. You can pray anytime, anywhere, still or active.

If you do not know who your guides are who walk with you, put the intention out there that you want to connect. Open your heart to communicate with them if you know who they are. You can make an offering at your place of prayer, light a candle, burn some incense, or do anything else that feels aligned.

Next, close your eyes and slow your breath. Breathe in deeply for five and breathe out for eight seconds. You can do this three times. Let your breath return to its natural rhythm, and focus on this for around three minutes. When ready, ask the questions you need support and guidance on. Thank them for their support.

Your answer may come straight away or over a few days. The answers will come in the form of *intuition*. Your answer may come to you in your environment, numbers or patterns, insight or inspiration, dreams, or through your inner senses or heart.

Trust your intuition, and trust it is perfectly safe for you to let the messages come through. Intuition will feel like an instinctual thought with a feeling around it. Keep your heart and mind open as your guides want to let you know you are supported and on the right path. Journal this experience and, moving forward, any others. You may want to refer back to them.

Visualisation

Everyone visualises whether we know it or not. We visualise in our dreams, in our daydreams, when we desire something or when we fear something. Yes, the "worst case scenario game" is a form of visualising too. We visualise when we set goals, run through our "to-do" lists when we make plans and do it day in and day out.

"Visualisation is the great secret of success"

Sandy Gallagher (1953 -)
American Author and creator of Proctor Gallagher Institute

If we were to look back on our lives and see our great achievements and failures, we would quickly see that we have visualised all of it. If you ask any successful person, they will tell you they saw themselves succeeding and imagined it.

Athletes use this technique all of the time. They run the game in their minds over and over and see themselves succeeding, whether winning or beating their personal best.

Visualisation takes practice, and meditations are a great way to exercise our minds. Our brain is like a muscle, and it needs using and training. I stand in front of my goal board every morning and evening, visualising each goal. I see the images in my mind, engage all of my senses, and make them as real as possible. Remember, our subconscious mind doesn't know if it is real, and it will make it happen. It took me a while to build this habit; I first needed to remember to do it. So I set alarms on my phone. I stand in front of my board in the kitchen, systematically read each goal and burn the image into my mind. I have ten goals, and I always keep them up to date. I have a written goal board and a visual one to assist me. I stand in front of the boards, read a goal, and then close my eyes. I focus on my breath, and then I start visualising. If my mind wanders, I look at the visual board and begin again. Through perseverance, I have reconditioned my mind and created new habit patterns.

It takes discipline to master visualisation and to co-create a paradise. The creative process is harnessing the power of our subconscious mind and being aware of our thought patterns through our emotions. Remember, we don't want a stream of negative thoughts and self-talk flowing through our minds unchecked and wreaking havoc. We can manage and keep track of our thoughts through our emotions and then channel this through visualisations. You become successful when you can confidently expect to receive what you have pictured. There can be no doubt. As we train our minds, doubt is replaced by expectancy. You need to live in this place, and then you'll be amazed at what you can create. If you have doubts, fear or negativity, that is OK, but learn to catch yourself and turn it into a positive.

Look at it this way, faith and fear require you to believe in something you cannot see. So why not choose faith, deliberately picture your dreams, and believe in the creative process?

Jax Emilio Robinson

https://linktr.ee/jax_lightlanguage

The Art of Imagination

I really wanted to name this segment the Art of Imagination rather than the Art of Visualization because there has always been a big part of me that has, first and foremost...IMAGINED my way to my dream life.

The concept of Visualisation was one that I was introduced to only a few years ago, to be honest. And to believe that it was the first time my brain collided with the concept - would be a lie. The word Visualisation is simply another way of saying Imagination. It just feels like more effort. It's the adult way of making a childhood gift feel harder.

I was imagining' from as young as I can remember. My fondest memories were from when I danced around our yard that surrounded our two-story home in Rural Queensland, Australia. This was the era where the Original Snow White and Cinderella movies headlined the Disney playlist. The era when films were watched by manually sliding a video tape into a VCR (Video Cassette Recorder). I recall my Mum's eagle eye, supervising the way to handle the video cassette, making sure we were gentle on the little snap-back flap that boarded the length of one of the brown edges.

Whilst dancing around the yard, I would sing at the top of my lungs while imagining being one of the Princesses.

I would kiss my imaginary prince.

I would sing to my imaginary mice.

I would live in my imaginary palaces.

I was none the wiser.

I would allow myself to lose my inhibitions just to inhibit this experience as a princess.

These were incredible moments for me. And when the Little Mermaid was released...well...I never left the pool that our Dad had installed one hot summer. I was Ariel forever...These moments were carved into my memory as an exceptional way to immerse myself into a world that helped me escape my reality. Especially during the times when my reality was hard. Particularly when I hit rock bottom in my early 30's.

See, life was fun. I spent most of my 20s running among lots of parties. Lots of travel. Honestly, I lived an amazing life that has curated cherished memories. But, of course, as life would have it, I experienced all of the ups and downs destined for me. But when I hit rock bottom in my 30s, the memories of accessing my Imagination became a catalyst of transformative change for me. So you could say my natural gift of Visualization was remembered through Imagination. And the great news is that we all have this gift!

Allow me to share with you what my rock bottom looked like. I met my first husband when I was 27.

We fell pregnant when I was 28.

At 30, we married.

At 32, we separated.

The years blessed us with owning and selling several homes, cars, businesses and 2 gorgeous children in the 5 years we were together.

He was a great man

An amazing Father

Still is an amazing Father

We were just not a match for the long term, and I have nothing but gratitude in my heart for his existence. During this time, though, as well as the emotional turmoil and weavings of heavy guilt and shame for ruining a marriage. I experienced traumatic grief and sadness when my Father, AND best friend both passed away in the space of 6 months. It was like being hit by 12 semi-trailer trucks while buried under a pile of bricks. It was excruciating. But I was so well trained to hold it all together. Kept it all together because I was running a business; I had to be the boss.

I had to know everything.

I had to keep my cool.

So like the good obedient student I was, I did was I was told Until…

I couldn't do it anymore.

The cracks started to reveal themselves in the shape of constant drinking and benders. I started to care less about the business and more about going clubbing. I started to care less about progressing and more about regressing. My motto at the time was, 'We're just going to die anyways', Which I wore like a badge of irresponsible honour.

I stopped caring…

And the bi-product of this was intense and irreversible.

Day by day, I started to lose everything.

Friends, Family, Money, Respect.

And the hard knock was...the business.

Which was my livelihood after leaving my husband.

I was left with nothing, Zilch.

No money

No income

No support

Cue in the gloomy rock bottom anthem... This was me for at least a year.

I was couch surfing. Bedroom dwelling as a guest in the home. And forever grateful for the help I received from so many beautiful people I crossed paths with. But the depth of darkness I experienced was the war that was going on in my head, The war that reminded me of how much of a failure I was.

The war shanked my worthiness at every chance it got. This is the war no one saw, but I certainly felt. With the help of google, I started researching ways to feel better... I was a constant heavy mess. I needed a way out of my head. And of course, as the Universe would it... Ask, and you shall receive. I was guided by the work and teachings of Abraham Hicks. A divine consciousness that speaks wisdom through a channeler named Esther Hicks. I was hooked, and I don't know why...

The teachings resonated as if I knew this information but somehow forgot.

And I had forgotten.

I learnt about the universal law of attraction. I learnt about

Visualisation.

I learnt about being the creator of our reality.

There were definitely a few hard truth pills that I didn't want to swallow, but eventually, I surrendered. I would take these teachings everywhere I went. I applied every subtle realization in moments no one saw. In fact, one of the most potent experiences I had was when I went for a walk down to the local lake and PRETENDED to present to an invisible audience. In this presentation – I was speaking as if I was in my future. I was sharing with this invisible audience that was soon joined by ducks paddling in the water how I actually overcame the rock bottom THAT I WAS IN!

I lost myself in this speech.

Just like when I did when I was a little girl.

I held an invisible Microphone.

I paced the staircase as if it were the stage.

I even answered questions!!!

And somehow I had all the answers!!! This exercise became so cathartic for me. I would often lose myself in the dream weaving of my future self. It was a process I enjoyed the feeling of. And over time, after having gradually studied the universal laws and the somatic impact our bodies have as co-creative devices. I discovered that this art form of Imagination was actually WORKING.

Fast forward 6 years from these moments on the stairs, and I AM LIVING MY BEST LIFE!!!

I public speak all the time. I share my story with a global audience that now learns these techniques from me; I facilitate transformative events and retreats.

I have attracted the love of my life

Every day is an exceptional day

And each day has been created from this unique foundation of LIVING in my Imagination paired with taking action from the energy of my future self!!! And it is my greatest honour and privilege to remind us all of this not-so-unique but very much underrated superpower we have access to IMAGINATION!!!

Jax

Focus on Breathing and how to Pay Attention

I want to share with you the tool of breathing. Taking soul cleansing breaths can help create new habits that can help us have the life we deserve. We all deserve a wonderful life. I do this technique for myself to maintain my sanity, my joy, and my drive. We don't just breathe to stay alive; we breathe to keep on top of our lives, stay standing on our foundations, and keep rising up.

When we feel fear, anxiety or stress, we tend to close up, our thoughts turn negative, and we dive into fight-flight mode. Our clarity becomes clouded, and we can make hasty decisions. In moments like these, all we need to do is breathe deeply. Yes, it's that simple. This slows the heart rate, levels the hormones, grounds us, and we feel a million times better. We fill our lungs with oxygen, calming our brain and nervous system. Your body works better in a calmer state. It keeps your immune system strong, your stomach and intestines working, and lowers blood pressure and heart rate. When we are in a better mindset, we can pay attention to the problem at hand and focus on the desired outcome. Remember, from earlier on, we cannot hold two thoughts simultaneously. We cannot experience fear at the same time as love.

"I admit thoughts influence the body."

Albert Einstein (1879 – 1955)

Theoretical Physicist

Many people live in fight-flight mode, which can have damaging impacts on their health. I know this through first-hand experiences. I had to relearn that my body is my temple. I can't go anywhere without it. Thoughts, intentions and emotions are not enough on their own. I need a body to take me there. So if you have thoughts racing through your head, breathe deeply. A balanced body will help you negotiate your way through your hardships.

We don't know what the future holds, so worrying about things that *"might"* happen is silly. You can deal with challenges when they occur and work towards the best outcomes. You need to pause, breathe deeply, and be conscious if you want to stop yourself from predicting your outcomes as negative ones. Take your post, for example; before you open that letterbox, pause, breathe deeply, and expect to find cheques and good news. Don't expect to see bills. You will have bills some days, and that's normal; it is a part of life. However, they will be expected rather than unexpected when you receive them.

There will be days when you open the mail in a hurry, and you will receive bad news or a bill. This highlights that you need time to refocus your mind, breathe and visualise, and focus on what you want.

Berenice Tan, founder of Karmably and Soulside Breathwork Facilitator Training, has an incredible knowledge of Breathwork. She explains how focusing on Breath can transform our lives and get off the hamster wheel.

"I love to win.

I love to grind, hustle and get it done.

I don't love feeling my whole body ache, getting sick, or scrolling mindlessly on social media to escape the suppressed feelings I avoided while I was in the DOING, DOING, DOING of it all.

But many find themselves stuck in a looping experience of Doing vs Being.

So...it isn't about learning to "let go" of Doing, or to even do less.

It's about CHANNELING our DOING.

Into more of what we love.

So the thrill of being in the masculine, becomes a Way of Being.

And allows the Inner Masculine to lead us to victory, without it being a hostile takeover!

... to dissolve the pattern and looping process of burnout and energetic overflow.

And replace it with integration, flow and total freedom in who you BE."

Berenice Tan (1987 -)

Breathwork Facilitator, Reiki, and Sound Therapist

Speaking to our Guides Exercise

This very simple breathing exercise can be done throughout the day. It can be done before business calls, meetings, stressful or anxiety-triggering situations, or even if your kids are driving you mad, and all you need is a minute to collect yourself.

No matter how you feel, where you are, or what you are doing, this exercise will help you ground yourself and reconnect you to the Divine.

Stand with your feet slightly apart, shoulders back and spine straight. As you breathe, stretch your arms and raise them above your head. Alternatively, hold your hand together as if in prayer, starting from the chest and raising them above your head, keeping your hands pressed together. Count to five as you are breathing in. Pause at the top for three seconds. As you breathe in, imagine roots growing from the ground into your feet and a deep red light travelling up the roots into you. Imagine this red light filling up your being as you breathe in. This is the red grounding light from our beautiful Mother Gaia.

Lower your arms or praying hands as you breathe outwards for eight seconds. Let them hang beside you loosely. Pause at the bottom of the breath for two seconds. As you breathe out, imagine a brilliant white, silver, or gold light coming down from the Divine and entering you through your Crown Chakra.

This light fills you and is in harmony with the red light.

Then repeat the exercise three times. How do you feel now?

"The Body Keeps the Score" – Trauma

I am sure many of you have heard this phrase and book called *"The Body Keeps the Score"* by Bessel Van Der Kolk (1943 -). Bessel Van Der Kolk is one of the world's leading experts on trauma. In his New York Times Bestseller, *"The Body Keeps the Score"* argues that trauma can cause devastating effects on the individual, their families and future generations. From thirty years of experience and research, it has been noted that trauma or traumas are stored in somatic memory. The individual then expresses this as changes in the biological stress response. Bessel Van Der Kolk is an inspiration as he boldly changes the paradigm of Western Culture, looking into alternative approaches to healing the body, mind, and brain.

Bessel Van Der Kolk offers to step away from conventional talking therapies and drug treatments. He looks at healing from trauma through:

- Owning yourself and being in control

- Speaking out loud your trauma, for silence leads to the death of the Soul

- Letting go of the past (EMDR)

- Learning to live in your body using Yoga

- Reforming your life through self-leadership

- Putting your memories back together

- Using Neurofeedback to rewire your brain

- Using facilities like theatres to find your voice

The brain is the most crucial organ. It is divided into the left hemisphere (controls the right side of the body) and the right hemisphere (controls the left side of the body). The Cerebellum is located at the lower back of the brain and comprises two hemispheres. This area controls digestion and heartbeat etc. The spinal cord connects the brain to the rest of the body. It travels down the entire length of the spine, and nervous systems branch off of it to the limbs and organs. The nerves feed information back to the brain, and the data is processed. We can act on information without needing to think about it. The nervous system is a complex system with many different components and elements. The nervous system is a communication system that controls the body. It allows your body to learn, walk, talk, breath, heartbeat etc. Your central nervous system is made up of your brain and spinal cord.

When we go through traumas, it is stored in our nervous system. Our mind cannot make sense of the event that has taken place, so the experience is not filed away correctly, with a date and time. We can start looping in that event or trauma with no beginning or end result. I suffered memory loss until I could face the events, speak to my Mum, who witnessed much of it, and go through the timelines from the beginning and through to the end. Journalling down the trauma was a way to express myself and match everything up safely. When it was down on paper, everything just seemed more manageable. But to get to this place, I had to feel physically safe. We cannot process trauma if we do not feel safe. We need to reestablish the feeling that we are in control and own our bodies and minds. We need to own our-self.

The next step is to learn coping mechanisms to remain calm when those feelings of rage, anger, becoming overwhelmed, shame or collapse. From there, we can remain calm when faced with the images, physical sensations, sounds or thoughts we meet from our trauma. Being in that state of calm can stop us from going into a state of hyper- and hypo-arousal. In these states, we cannot process anything properly, and unwanted images and sensations flood our brains. As a result, we can become disorientated, confused, angry, fearful, and disconnected from our bodies. In a state like this, we cannot learn, and the connection between our logical (conscious) and emotional brain (subconscious) is thrown out of sync. The neuroscientist Joseph LeDoux (1949 -) has shown that self-awareness is the only way to reconnect the two.

We can only change our feelings by becoming aware of our inner experiences. We can explore this through journalling, meditation, breathing, chanting, yoga, and mindfulness.

Person-centred counselling was incredibly helpful in starting me on this journey. By feeling the unbearable sensations, we begin to heal. The unbearable becomes bearable. Not wanting to feel uncomfortable emotions makes us feel overwhelmed. Feeling physically calm while accessing the fear and trauma is essential to recovery. And to clarify, you can feel physically calm and have a good cry. I was relaxed, feeling all the things I feared to feel, but I cried and cried and cried. I let it all out. The tears rolled down my face, and I was calm.

There are many famous stories and legends that are about facing your fears and finding your salvation through healing your traumas. The King Arthur story describes a scene where he is sitting at the round table with his Knights, and they are searching for the Holy Grail. This can be seen as a psychological statement, as the quest is a place of finding redemption. The Holy Grail represents a connection to the Divine through transcending and ascending to a higher plane of consciousness. King Arthur tells his knights that they must go to the Forest, find the place darkest to them and start looking there, and there they will find the Holy Grail.

The award-winning original Netflix series *"Stranger Things"* has countless examples where the characters need to go to where the monsters live to find their true selves. Through facing fears and the forces of evil, the innocence of childhood shine and they find their true authentic selves while travelling the road of hope. To conquer fear, they must soften their hardened hearts and study their relationships, love for others, and, of course, themselves. The only true evil comes from a lack of love, but when there is a balance of masculine bravado and feminine insight (recognise this Universal Law?), either within a character or within a group, hope and love prevail.

Harry Potter is another excellent example. When Harry is looking for the Philosopher's Stone, he must journey to all the places he doesn't want to. Harry needs to go to the basement under the castle, where the Basilisk lives. He must face the giant scary monsters and face his fears to conquer them. The Philosopher's Stone appears in his pocket when Harry looks into the mirror, sees his deceased parents, and meets his fear of grief and loss. When Harry faces the trauma of losing his parents, the trauma dissipates.

These stories show that when we face our trauma, there is no traumatic battle. Nothing is conquered. There is no victory. There is love, salvation, tenderness, care, balance, openness, spaciousness, transcendence, renewal, compassion, release, letting go and many feelings. Freeing trauma can be so freeing in a tender, compassionate way.

"We can hardly bear to look. The shadow may carry the best of the live we have not lived. Go into the basement, the attic, the refuse bin. Find gold there. Find an animal who has not been fed or watered. It is you!! This neglected, exiled animal, hungry for attention, is a part of yourself."

Stephen Cope (1977 -)

Psychotherapist, Kripalu Yoga Teacher, and Author

Releasing Trauma Exercise

This exercise is for those who want to let go of anything that no longer serves them a purpose. This could be traumas or any memories you do not like facing.

Pick one of the following, or do as many as you want.

Journal your experiences afterwards

Burning Ceremony: As a family or individually, find items that represent trauma, addiction problems, egos or anything else. Burn them (safely) as a way of letting go and grieving.

Timelines: This worked very well for me. As a family or individually, write your timelines for the events. Compare this timeline with others to see how the trauma affected everyone and fill in the missing blanks. If you suffer from memory loss, this can form a beginning, middle and end. If anyone has addiction problems, you can identify where this occurred concerning the trauma.

I'll keep you safe ritual: If appropriate, your parents can do an *"I'll keep you safe"* ritual. This is where you can be held by your parents or each other, and they can express how they want to keep you safe. Finish the ritual by saying, "I'll keep you safe for as long as you allow me to." This can be a very emotional ritual where love and forgiveness can blossom.

Revisiting Trauma Sites: This can be done with the family or individually (with/without a therapist). Revisit the site where the trauma occurred and feel the rising emotions. Feel the hurt, blame, sadness, grief, shame, anger, pain, fear, or other feelings that arise. Sit with these emotions. Release them, and start the healing by leaving symbols of love and peace. These can include letters to the trauma, flowers, a white ribbon representing "peace" or "serenity", homemade cocoons, chalk drawings or letting go of biodegradable balloons. The family embracing and making commitments to each other is an excellent form of healing and validation. If you are there alone, make commitments to yourself.

Symbolic Transformation: Challenge yourself to identify and implement ways to transform toxic and self-harming habits. You can do this with family, a close friend, a therapist or other forms of support. Look at any behaviour that is unhealthy and harmful to yourself, and see how you can change these habits. To signify your commitment to change, you might want to decorate your home/bedroom, rearrange furniture, clear old clothes you do not wear and donate them to charity, have a haircut, learn a new skill, join a club or anything else that comes to mind.

Trauma and Forgiveness

With healing from trauma comes forgiveness. You feel you need to forgive yourself, or you may feel like you need to forgive parents, family members, or anyone who was the aggressor.

Through my journey of domestic abuse, fleeing abuse, and all the stuff that came after, I discovered many more layers under "rock bottom". I cried more tears than I thought possible. At first, the shame consumed me. When the healing started, it was rough. I had eighteen sessions with a counsellor, and this helped tremendously. But there is only so much a counsellor can do. I needed to do the rest. Healing from trauma is not all rainbows and cupcakes. It is facing your deepest darkest place and having to remember. It is needing to piece things back together again. It is having to rewire your brain, reconnect with your body, find that inner child and sMother them with love and compassion. Healing from trauma is about being vulnerable, pulling yourself off the floor, and starting to walk forward. Unfortunately, I cannot share my full story of domestic abuse as I would end up in court for defamation of character. Some other factors were at play, and I truly *hated* myself for ending up in that situation.

Before thinking about forgiveness towards my former partner and his family, I had to forgive myself. I had to work through the shame and the guilt. It took me several years to get to this place, where I genuinely hold myself with compassion. So the time came when the traumas were nearly healed, but one piece of the puzzle was missing. It has taken me two years to find peace, and I only achieved that through forgiveness. I'll explain whatever we put out into the Universe and we receive back through the natural laws, remember chapter two? When I sent my ex hatred, resentment, fear, anger and hurt, I received that back. The love and peace I was attracting were limited because I sent these other toxic negative feelings into the Universe. I was harming myself by hating him with every ounce of my being. When I discovered what it is to forgive genuinely, a whole avalanche of excellent opportunities came my way. My ex is still attempting to control me and sending a lot of hatred my way. It's not getting to me, as it's being returned to him (through the law of attraction). The love and forgiveness I send out to him are being returned to me. So by sending him positive, powerful emotions, I am protecting and loving myself, my family and my friends. This is how I have found a deep sense of divine peace and a love worthy of me. This is how I healed from years of trauma.

Chapter Six

Major Emotions

We will explore our emotions in this chapter, starting with the negative ones.

Major Negative Emotions

Nearly all of our primary negative emotions stem from just one: fear. The list is endless: doubt, worry, criticism, judgement, abandonment. These emotions all stem from fear. We will look at negative emotions through the eyes of fear, and then you can workshop them in your journal. It would help if you thought about other emotions: hatred, superstition, revenge, anger and jealousy. Do you feel any of these? Feel free to journal these after you have worked through the fear-based ones.

Fear

Do not run from fear! We have been conditioned to do this our whole lives. We have never been taught to face it. Fear is like a black hole. It emits no light and reflects no light. But fear can suck you in when you get too close, and it can become the engine of the most powerful events in our lives. I used to fear being loved because I only knew the lack of love for so long. I didn't want people to fall in love with me. It made me feel uncomfortable, which was a reflection of myself. I needed to *love* myself first before allowing anyone else to love me. You need to *listen* to fear and hear what is being said. *Then* we can move on from it. Fear is just an emotion, just like love is. What is this emotion telling us? Is it giving us information by telling us to study more, wake up earlier, get some help, or slow down? When we listen to fear, we tune into our intuition, and we can work through the emotion. Running from fear gets us nowhere.

So what emotions are born from fear? There are many examples, but let's name a few and journal these emotions in our journals. Then, if the fear is irrelevant to you, consider what it might mean to someone else.

Negative Emotions

Doubt: We feel doubt when we are disconnected from our gut feeling. Doubt stems from the fear of the unknown. There is uncertainty, indecision, and hesitation. What do you doubt?

Worry: Some people worry more than others. I used to worry until I learnt about the Laws of the Universe and the power of prayer. I know people who worry about everything and some who only worry *"when it is time to worry"*. My Mum was a big worrier until I taught her about the power of prayer. Prayer evaporated a large chunk of her worry. Worry causes anxiety and causes you to obsess over the "what if's". What do you worry about? What type of worrier are you?

Rejection: Rejection essentially means hearing the word *"no"*. This powerful little word needs to be used more! When we start saying *no* more and *yes* less, we take the fear out of rejection. It also makes our "yes" much more powerful. What do you first think or feel when you see this word?

The unknown: When you think about it, our whole future is the unknown. It is like driving through the night with our headlights on. You can travel vast distances by only seeing what a few feet in front of you is. Every time you step into the unknown, the next step is revealed. The unknown is not knowing the outcome of a situation. Your comfort zone kills your dreams, and your success lies on the other side of your comfort zone. Are you the type of person who wants to know the outcome before you commit? If someone offered you a new job or a business proposal, would you turn it down because it is the unknown? Do you play a worst-case scenario game or keep positive if unsure about an outcome?

Commitment: This doesn't just come into play in your relationships but in all areas of your life, including yourself. Are you committed to freedom? Or are you committed to scarcity and lack?

Being wrong: I see many teenagers with this fear! Where is this fear coming from? Is it something you can relate to? Or do you see mistakes as an opportunity to learn? If we are wrong, does that make us *bad* in some way? Is it a fear of how we are going to be perceived if we are wrong rather than being wrong?

Conflict: I used to struggle with this fear. I was a complete and utter people-pleaser. I used to avoid contact at all costs. I never wanted an argument, and the thought of conflict used to make my heart race, my cheeks would blush, I would get red patches all over my neck and chest, and my hands would get clammy. I would say yes to things I didn't want to do to avoid that awkward feeling, which looped back around to not having self-love and giving my power away.

Failure: We have this fear rammed down our throats in school! And for some, in home life. You must consistently achieve, can't fail, and pass every exam and homework assignment. We fear failure because of the expectations of others placed on us, and then we place those expectations on ourselves.

Poverty: This is a place no one wants to be. It is a place of lack and scarcity. I have had to go to the food bank several times before, and standing in that queue, I felt shame. I have had to rely on people giving me items I needed, and I have had to decide whether to turn the heating on. I had opened my fridge many times before, and there was nothing apart from some apples, milk, soya milk and a couple of yoghurts. At times like these, I used to look at my son and promise we would never be that poor again. It wasn't the abundant life we ALL deserve to have. Some of you may be thinking, if everyone can have infinite abundance, won't things just run out? The answer is no. We all don't want the same things. You can't sit and wait for things to get better, you have to decide what you want, and then the Universe will conspire to make it happen.

Abandonment: I have had many times in my life where I felt this feeling, mostly around relationships. My son felt it the first few times he was left at a childminder and nursery.

Spotlight: I used to hate the spotlight! When I was younger, I didn't want to get married because I didn't want to be the centre of attention. Today I see many others who do not like the limelight, and I respect that. I interview many people for my podcast; some people do not want their faces seen, so it is an audio interview. I like to video record interviews so I can use them on YouTube and the Apple Podcast. It is so important to respect the other person's boundaries.

Success: People who fear success have a similar fear of money. People undervalue themselves and underperform, so they don't meet the next version of themselves. They fear that they might lose everything the minute they succeed. Or they fear they will lose their loved ones if they succeed. They may worry if they are successful, people won't like them anymore, and they like the success instead.

Judgement: As Lisa Nichols says, other people's opinions of you are not your business. When we fear judgement, we do not step into our full power. When we fear judgement, we are giving our power away. This fear can be so intense for some that they make themselves small and shrink. As a Witch, I face a lot of judgement and discrimination just because people fear the unknown. My faith is misunderstood because of the Media, Films, TV series, etc. I worship Nature, and that is how simple it gets to be! I understand now that if people judge, then they have many internal things going on, and it's about them, not me.

Ill health: The fear of ill health is very much linked to the fear of old age and death. Fear causes ill health, as it puts unnecessary stress on the body. Fear of ill health also ties into money fears. Ill health is expensive! It is cheaper to pay for a healthy lifestyle than for ill health.

Old age: People who usually fear old age fear death. Old age brings us a step closer to death. It is essential to remember you are only as old as you feel.

Death: Death is nothing to fear! People who fear death fear the unknown. It is seen simply as the next step in our journey when we understand that we have a life after death. We are energy, and energy can neither be created nor destroyed.

Loss: This fear is wide-reaching. People fear losing wealth, money, loved ones, their life, possessions, status, relationships, jobs, and the list can go on. Do you fear loss? How would losing something valuable to you feel? How would it impact your day or life?

Money: We are going to workshop this fear in the next activity

The only real fear is the fear we are born with, and you might be surprised there are only two fears wired into our DNA. The two fears are the fear of falling and the fear of loud sounds. Every other fear is *learnt*. Every other negative emotion stems from fear.

Reactions to Fear Exercise

Feel free to journal your reactions to fears in your journal, and think about how you will shift this dense energy blockage. Think about your Chakras and The Natural Laws of the Universe; think about any traumas which might have created this fear. Where does the fear stem from? How do you clear and free it? You have all of the tools you need! Tune into your body and listen to that small, powerful voice.

Overcoming Money Fear

Money is a conversation that we need to talk about more. We navigate money with a mountain of emotions and don't discuss it. Money carries many of our fears. The fear of not having enough, the fear of debt, the fear of loss and the fear of not having money and needing it. There is so much fear around money because we are in serious trouble without it. The flip side of the coin is that we have tons of money, but we are fearful people only like us for our money, and not us! It's time to talk about something other than the struggle. Let's talk about wealth building, hope, contentment, happiness and abundance. There is so much energy around money because money is an energy, and money is a masculine energy.

Men find it much easier to talk about money than women unless they have been taught about money. Women can feel out of their depths and unsure how to tackle the conversation. Here are some tips for creating abundance. Abundance is for everyone, but how do we accomplish this? Firstly we follow the universal laws and do that inner work on ourselves. Secondly, we need to understand that where we are financially did not happen overnight, and where we are going won't happen overnight, but we can be consistent in our change and growth. You are where you are now because of your previous mindset.

Money, finance and wealth are all under the same umbrella, but they are their unique elements. You need to start separating them in your mind and tackle them individually. You can have money and struggle, and you can have finances to navigate and still wonder if you will have enough money to make it to the end of the month. You can have wealth and still be sad, have ill health or not live in abundance.

We must be clear that money does not change who you are and shouldn't be given enough power to do this. I know there is a lot of fear around this alone; I used to feel it, too. We created money to serve us. It was designed as an exchange system. In the past, we used livestock, goods, silver, and gold as our exchange currency. Now we have money. When facing problems, it is better to do it with money, as money allows you to navigate and gives you more freedom. Money gives you the freedom to live the life of your dreams and to create good memories. Cash enables you to solve problems for your family and yourself, and it allows you to support your community.

Most of us come into this world with a fear block around money passed down by our grandparents and parents. We shouldn't give money away, we should save money, we should guard money, and we shouldn't talk about money. Let's talk money! Money talk is where your tribe comes into play. Find someone who knows more about money than you do. Do not learn from someone who is no good with money! They must have an understanding. I watch Youtube channels like Lisa Nichols and Bob Proctor. They openly share their knowledge and have videos dedicated to specific topics.

Keeping the Laws of the Universe in mind, think of money like this; If you keep hold of your money and don't circulate it, then your wealth will be limited. You need to circulate money freely, as that is what it was designed for. The minute you put money in a tin or a box, it becomes useless. Think about your intentions behind money

I know this might seem like a silly thing to say, but get Life Insurance! When writing this book, mine was seven pounds a month, and I knew my son would be provided for if anything happened to me. There is no other way to replace your income if something happens to you! Where would that leave your family? Whether you own a house or not, get life insurance.

I used to turn off the minute my Dad or my Mum asked me if I was saving money. I never had enough money left over to put into a savings account! Bob Proctor changed my whole view on this. He called savings *"paying yourself"*. I *loved* that idea, which shifted the fear of not having enough to save, the fear of being unmanageable, and the fear of failure! In his book *"You Were Born Rich",* he suggests paying yourself *first*, before any bills. That intention of paying yourself is a seed being planted, and the Universe hears it. It is the Babylonian Law of success. Ask anyone who is financially successful how they became successful, and they will tell you this is what they did. So the question is, how much do you save? The answer is ten per cent of your earnings. I couldn't manage this for a while, so I started with five per cent and then worked my way up to ten per cent. Do not save for "a rainy day" because this is what you will attract. Please save your money to invest it into something later on. Please only put your savings into an account you don't have easy access to, as this will prevent you from being tempted to use it too easily.

Debt. That word stinks of fear! It even sounds like a horrible word. I used to be in thousands of pounds worth of debt. What do we do with debt? We face it just like we face our fears. Talk to someone who knows how you can be helped. Many agencies can help you come up with a Debt repayment plan. I used to try and hide from my Debt. Sounds silly, right? I would never look at credit card statements, and I stopped budgeting when I thought it was hopeless. Again Bob Proctor changed how I felt and thought of the Universal Laws, and I made a considerable effort to start managing it responsibly. Bob Proctor furthermore suggests that twenty per cent of your earnings should go towards paying off debt. It may sound like a lot, but remember, some agencies can help consolidate or retire them. It will take you longer to pay back, but at least they are being paid off. If finances are not your strong point, it is important to find a competent financial counsellor who can teach you. The rest of your money can go to yourself and paying bills. Mortgages should not be seen as a dept but as an investment. When you have your cash budgeted out, your stress levels will reduce, and you can start thinking about abundance rather than lack and scarcity.

So what have we accomplished?

We have a savings account with regular money for future investments.

Your debt problems are sorted and being paid off.

You have around seventy per cent left to go on the house, family and anything else.

If you are serious about earning big money in the future, you need to get a hold of the concept of managing it now. This intention of managing your money will be sent off into the Universe, and abundance will be returned to you.

Two books I highly recommend reading are:

Lynne Twist's *"The Soul of Money"*

and

Amanda Francis's *"Rich As Fuck"*

Major Positive Emotions

Love is the most powerful positive emotion, followed by sex, desire, faith, gratitude, hope (hope conquers fear), enthusiasm, happiness, excitement, joy, serenity, creativity, pride, and romance. Of course, many more positive emotions exist, but we will focus on these.

Two emotions cannot be felt simultaneously, and our bodies might switch rapidly between positive and negative ones, but we can hold one at a time. Our thoughts and feelings must be predominantly positive to create a life full of abundance, wealth and happiness. It is normal to feel negative emotions and remember the Laws of the Universe, but it's important to catch yourself and change this. Work through your feelings head-on, and use your body as a tool to help you. This is the only way to change your paradigm and subconscious mind.

We are to workshop these positive emotions in our journal:

Major Positive Emotions Exercise

In your journal, describe in detail what makes you feel the following emotions. What situations are currently happening in your life that makes you feel these positive emotions? If you struggle to think of something, think about the small things too. Sometimes we overlook the small moments because we are always wanting more.

"And above all, watch with glittering eyes the whole world around you because the greatest secrets are always hidden in the most unlikely places. Those who don't believe in magic will never find it."

Roald Dahl (1916 – 1990)

British Novelist

Love

Sex

Desire

Faith

Gratitude

Hope

Enthusiasm

Happiness

Excitement

Joy

Serenity

Creativity

Pride

Romance

Now I want you to write a paragraph (or two) describing your dream life in as much detail as possible, using the above emotions as keywords.

How does that *feel*!? Do you feel the *visualisation*? Do you feel your *vibration rise*? Do you feel *good*? Feel it as if you *already* have it. Feel as if you are *already living it*. If you still need to do so, I invite you to make a vision board with everything you have described and hang it where you can see it. Then, each morning bring yourself back to this moment and feel as if it has already happened. Remember, if you do not know what you want, how can you ask for it?

"A thankful person is thankful under all circumstances. A complaining soul complains even in paradise."

Bahá'u'lláh (1817–1892)

Prophet-founder of the Bahá'í Faith

Causes of Failure

The leading cause of failure is that people start off well, but they don't see instant results, so they say, *"this doesn't work"*, and they give up. No one knows how long something will take, but if you practice the different techniques in this book, you will see results in thirty days. When you change your mindset, your whole life will change.

Let's look at other reasons people fail to manifest true abundance in all areas of their lives. Remember the first chapter about the mind, where I wrote about how we learn? We learn through constant repetition, which doesn't change as we age. Some people think if they read something one time or they listen to a YouTube video, they have suddenly changed their paradigm. It takes constant repetition of the same idea to change your paradigm, just like when we were children. I have listened to all my heroes over and over and over again. I played audiobooks on repeat and watched the same YouTube videos countless times. I have watched *"The Secret"* film by Rhonda Byrne around twenty times. And by the way, I'm not a headphone type of girl (I can't hear my child with massive noise reducers on), so Harrison listened with me. If you have a family or partner, even better! Change their paradigm too! Let the whole family join in! We must expose ourselves to new ideas to replace the old ones in our subconscious. We can create new habits aligned with our desired outcomes by impressing this idea into our minds.

Success is a committed decision. Many people fail at the first hurdle because they need clarification on what they want. Some people are fantastic at gathering information but fail to put it into practice. There are so many intelligent people, but they are penniless because they do not apply their knowledge to change their life. I know many *"certificate collectors"* who complete course after course but never actually do anything with what they have learnt. The minute they have finished one course, they are enrolled on another. Always the student, but never the master. It doesn't matter how smart you are; your paradigm still controls you!

"Knowledge is a treasure, but practice is the key to it."

Ibn Khaldun (1332-1406)
Arab Sociologist, Philosopher, and Historian

You will only succeed if you know where you are and where you are going.

"Success is the progressive realization of a worthy ideal."

Earl Nightingale (1921-1989)
American Radio Speaker and Author

Quantum Leaps: The Uncommon Sense

My Hero on quantum leaps is Price Pritchett, who wrote the groundbreaking book "*You2*". He is one of the bestselling authors in the world, with over twenty million copies in print.

I got to a point where I just experienced sheer frustration on a day-to-day basis. Then it hit me, and I told my Tribe, *"my yesterday's behaviour, mindset, bank account, health etc., don't fit today and definitely won't fit tomorrow. I am ready for my next level! Even though I have no idea what it looks like, I want to take a leap of faith and jump."* The jump is the quantum leap. Choosing a different set of risks is a quantum leap; it goes against our fear barriers and breaks through them. You can physically react when you push through the fear, into the unknown, with nothing but faith that the next step will be shown. This second change the paradigm and creates new evidence.

You can never escape risks, and there is always something at "*risk*". It is not something you can choose to live without, but you can risk believing in yourself and choose what risks you are willing to take. Please don't get in the way of yourself by overcomplicating and overthinking things; it doesn't need to be *complicated.*

"Trying harder" isn't necessarily the solution to achieving more. It may not offer any real promise for getting what you want out of life. Sometimes, in fact, it's a big part of the problem.

If you stake your hopes for a breakthrough on trying harder than ever, you may kill your chances for success"

Price Pritchett (1941 -)

American Author

If you genuinely want to succeed, you must change your game plan. Whatever you have been doing up till now may not be working, or it could work better. Doing *more* of whatever you have been doing isn't the answer. More of the same and trying harder can only lead you in one direction, burnout. Therefore doing more damage than good. You need to stop going with the obvious, get uncomfortable, and do something different, and you don't need a step-by-step plan. A quantum leap means going forward with no roadmap but focusing on the result. Visualisation is key. Visualise success, and you will achieve it. The Universe will sort out the how. If things fail, see the failures as an opportunity to learn, and learn your limits, then ask for help and carry on.

Never give up because you will succeed! You are, after all, a unique expression of the Universe.

Chapter Seven

The Magic of Relationships and Sex

We need to get clear on relationships first. I mean a relationship with everyone, including ourselves. To experience *pleasure*, we need to love *ourselves* first. And not in the way you are probably thinking.

Love Yourself First

Loving yourself at first may be a difficult thing to do. I found it very difficult. I had to get to know the true authentic me. I had to look in the mirror, I had to look myself straight in the eye, and I had to accept what I saw. We are ever-evolving and ever-changing. Who we were five years ago is different from who we are today. And who we are in five years is different than today. So right now, at this moment, you are one hundred per cent complete. Other people cannot complete you, and you complete yourself. And *only* you. If you are in a relationship or looking for one, where you expect the other person to complete you, you aren't going to get very far. A relationship is designed to complement your company. And once this is achieved, you can attract someone who loves you equally.

How do you completely accept yourself? You can only wholly accept yourself through love and acceptance, so there is no guilt or shame. Guilt and shame are holding you back and dragging you down. You cannot create a future full of abundance when you have those two emotions shackled around your ankles.

"All that we are is the result of what we have thought."

The Buddha

Religious Teacher

In your journals, I want you to confront the shame and the guilt. Jax Robinson and Lisa Nichols inspired me to work through mine.

The first two questions Jax Emilio Robinson asked me were:

What are you ashamed of?

What are you sorry for?

I have added my first response to these two questions from the 13th of September 2022 below.

What are you ashamed of?

I am ashamed that I never fought back, I am so embarrassed that I never stood up for myself, and I am so sorry that I just took the abuse from my former abusive partner. I am ashamed that I never found my voice and spoke my true feelings. I was so worried I would hurt HIS feelings. I am sorry that I let his opinions affect my body image that I had for myself. I am ashamed that I lacked courage. If I had spoken up, if I had screamed, if I had shouted, if I had fought, if I had valued myself as a person, the abuse would never have gone on for so long. I am ashamed that I let him put me in an invisible prison. I am ashamed that I wasn't stronger. I am embarrassed that I didn't know how to love myself.

What are you sorry for?

I am so sorry that I lost years of happiness and that I suffered so much.

I am so sorry that I don't listen to my body. I am sorry that I am careless with it. I'm sorry that I don't always understand its language. I'm sorry that I ignore the pain and I don't rest when it's tired. I'm sorry I don't feed and hydrate it properly. I'm sorry I don't give it time to heal. I'm so sorry that I don't always feel comfortable in it. I'm sorry, I don't know how to rest.

I'm sorry for sometimes telling people messages I know they aren't ready to hear. I'm sorry I get impatient with them and say things I then regret because I know it has triggered them. And I'm sad because I know it reflects how I treat myself.

I can tell you, tears were streaming down my face as I wrote those sentences. What a release it was. To finally confront it, to finally acknowledge it, and to finally feel it dissipate. Just by acknowledging it, I could feel the healing flowing in. I didn't have to *do* anything. I could just *be*. I cried off and on for around a week, and I didn't hold the tears back. Each time I felt a wave, I just cried it out. It felt wonderful afterwards! I also felt emotionally exhausted, but that feeling didn't last long. The exhaustion came from releasing so much and finally being free of that weight. I had never felt so much before! Now, this is not the same feeling as burnout. No way! It is the complete opposite and a sense of transformation and renewal. It was a Holy Grail feeling.

Holy Grail Exercise

Now it's your turn. In your Journal, answer these two questions:

What are you ashamed of, past and present?

What are you sorry for, past and present?

I want you to finish now these sentences inspired by Lisa Nichols' mirror talk, and I want you to have ten different reasons for each one, speak to yourself as if you were speaking to your closest friend:

You are worthy of,

I forgive you for,

I promise to,

How do you feel now? It is a good idea to repeat this exercise as frequently as possible.

Relationships Are Mirrors

To manifest our dream lives and have true abundance and wealth, we must be clear in our relationships. Not just with others but with ourselves too.

How do we do this?

You must first understand your energy signature to connect you to the energy signature of the Divine so you can live your life of true abundance. When you start exploring and learning about your unique energy signature, you begin experiencing your aligned, true, authentic self. When you understand *you*rself, you can begin harnessing your powers. You can take your control back, and this is the Holy Grail, for the Holy Grail is liberation.

The first step is to list the relationships that are not one hundred per cent in any shape or form. It can feel intense when we free ourselves from the shackles of an old narrative or paradigm. We no longer need to carry the labels we place on other people. When we label and judge someone, we are labelling and judging ourselves. We need to see ourselves as "*neutrality*". The feeling of contentment and gratitude is the feeling of the Divine, which brings sensations of bliss, transcendence and ascension. Clearing energy and creating space in a relationship need to be seen as an opportunity to understand ourselves better.

When a relationship is not one hundred per cent, it means

something is happening inside us. It means we have energy blockages or dense energy that needs shifting. You might be wondering how a relationship is a reflection of ourselves. Relationships are everything and have the power to cause war or peace. Relationships are the mirrors of core wounds within ourselves that have remained neglected and unhealed. Relationships are crucial because we are all one.

"We are only ever mirrors of each other."

Jax Emilio Robinson (1983 -)

Entrepreneur, LIFE Wealth Mentor

Labelling Exercise

We are going to do this in baby steps.

Firstly list all of the relationships that are not one hundred per cent.

Secondly, list all of the labels you have given everyone and yourself, for example, race, gender, class, and sexual orientation-based labels or labels such as: bright, wealthy, stylish, talented, popular, famous, bully, people pleaser, evil, monster, parent, addict, single Mum, loner etc.

When you start seeing yourself as a vibrational being and not a piece of meat walking around, you will truly liberate your life and create a life of abundance. We spoke about Universal Laws in chapter two, and I encourage you to reread this chapter.

How do we shift energy?

Blocked or dense energy is felt in the body as a tension point. You will *feel* the energy blockage. You will feel it in your muscles, in your stomach, in your heart, and your aura. In a Tarot Reading, a blocked energy point will come up as a card reversed (upside down). We have to be conscious of how we feel moving forward and consciously bring the tension points to the surface. If someone *triggers* you, then this is a tension point. We need to make a choice to see relationships as mirrors and feel into that. When we behave the same way we always have, we cannot create a happy, abundant future if we keep operating in the past. We are not just imagining a better future but *feeling* it. Nothing in our external environment can liberate us. Only our internal environment can liberate us.

Do we need to ask ourselves where we are experiencing separation? Separation is a dense, heavy closed feeling. Liberation is openness and love. The creative principle is feeling the paradigm at the moment and *not* repeating the pattern or the past. The creative principle creates new paradigms, evidence, and behaviour patterns. We can learn many skills that enable us to change our paradigm in the moment. Meditation is one of them, but remember, these skills, such as meditation, are a practice because it isn't the real thing!

Meditation is the sensation of mastering our emotions, so when we are in crisis or stressed, we can apply our practice and master our emotions at *that* moment, at the moment that counts. To do something new and not repeat the past. For example: When your child is screaming, and you want to scream into a pillow, when you are experiencing road rage, when you are sitting in a court room wanting to vomit, when you are about to have complete memory loss in an exam, that is when the practice of mediation matters! So we can feel the feelings and remain calm and not lose it.

You are Responsible for your Emotions

You are entirely and wholly responsible for your own life, experiences, emotions and outcomes. No other being on this planet is responsible for how you feel. There is no being on this planet that has the power to control how you feel. You have decided to feel every single emotion that you have ever felt. You need to accept this, or you will remain a victim of the illusion that everyone else is responsible for how you feel.

Relationships are mirrors of ourselves. What we see in others is what is reflected in us. The only way you are going to explore this is through creating new evidence and changing your paradigm. The only way we experience separation from the Divine is caused through experiencing separation narratives in our relationships. We are all connected, so separation doesn't technically exist, but we are not connected if we believe that we are separate from everyone else. Ring a bell? The

Universal Law of Mentalism speaks of this.

How does it feel if I was to say a child is not separate from you? A four-year-old is not separate from you. How does that feel? If we come from the same source, we are all the same age. We are just experiencing different timelines. Co-creation is oneness with all. Separation is self-centred and blocks abundance.

Look at your relationship with yourself, home life, business, and every part of your life. Ask the question, what was that feeling? Why did I feel like that? Why did I just put myself down? Why did I shrink? Why did I feel repressed? We can only match the frequency we desire when we expand our frequency with openness. We anchor ourselves to old narratives and closed relationships with ourselves or others and then try to match our new frequency. We *"try"*. When we clear this space and become an energetic match to what we want, we reach our desires with no effort through openness and truthfulness. Being open and truthful in a relationship may feel like a considerable risk! We have all this fear that we hold onto, fear we hurt the other persons feeling, fear of rejection, fear of abandonment. Anxiety, worry, fear. But risks and bold moves always pay off. Every risk-taking or bold move reveals the next step. If we don't know the way, the Universe will show us through the act of being truthful.

Relationship Exercise

Starting with three relationships, clear the space. Then move on to the next three and so forth, which could be relationships from the past or in the present. I invite you to call, voice note, text or write a letter to them from your heart. Hold no fear and tell them exactly how you feel. If the person cannot be contacted, or it is not safe to do so, or they are deceased, write a letter. Put the intention out to the Universe with the knowledge we are all connected, and on a Soul level, they will receive the message.

I want you to:

Communicate without blame, judgement, resentment, fear and any other negative emotions

Share truthfully with an open heart

Have no attachments to their response, and continue to soften, be even more open, and more loving

Make peace with any outcome knowing that what will be will be. If you are meant to be in each other's lives, you will be reconnected when the time is right.

Remember what we want to see in others; we must find it in ourselves first. When someone abuses us, it isn't easy to move past that at first, especially if it's someone we are meant to feel safe with. For example, I ended up being abused because I lacked love for myself, confidence and self-esteem, and I didn't know how to feel present in my body due to living in chronic pain. I, therefore, attracted an abuser: someone who didn't love me and amplified all of my other self-negative thoughts. Then the cycle of attracting more abuse continued until I fled.

In complicated situations where children are abused, the abuser is doing the abuse to harm themselves. There has been a lot of research into this, and it is thought that the perpetrator cannot engage with their emotions, and they hurt others to feel something in themselves. Many perpetrators of abuse, murder or rape experienced childhood traumas. They may have faced family dysfunction, emotionally distant or absent parents, or physical or sexual abuse. It does not excuse their behaviour, but sometimes it can help us understand why it happened. People are not born "*evil*"; their environments and relationships shape them. We looked at this in detail in chapter one. My former partner had a long list of mental health problems that I didn't want to accept. I just saw him as a *cruel, evil* person. From studying counselling, I came to understand that it was likely he had a narcissistic personality disorder. The term narcissistic has become a trend, and every former partner is an alleged narcissist. It is not a trend but a severe disorder. The overuse and misuse of the word have now caused actual harm to those with a narcissistic personality disorder.

I choose to love and forgive, not hate. This attitude seemed alien to many people, and I even had comments saying, "well, the abuse couldn't have been *that* bad if you can forgive him". The abuse was soul-breaking, and it took me years to forgive. But I had to forgive *myself* first, and this is how we live in love.

"I hear many speak about changing a paradigm in concept but without the substance of realising that we can only change our own paradigm to impact the entire paradigm. And changing it simply means to choose LOVE in situations that we as a society justify to LOVE LESS..."

Jax Emilio Robinson (1983 -)
Entrepreneur, LIFE Wealth Mentor

Sex Magick

Imagine two people sitting together eating an intimate dinner for two, candles lit, flowers, a couple of glasses of wine, and music playing softly in the background. It might shock you, but this represents a Wiccan (Witches) ritual. This is, in fact, a celebration of the Feminine. Wine, flowers and food are offerings to the Goddess, and the candles represent a place for magic, a sacred place. Candlelight creates the effect of neither light nor dark but the area in between.

Pre-Christian Europe celebrated sex and sexuality, which was considered natural, healthy and desirable. Men and women were not judged or held in contempt for their sexual desires or sexual preferences. Homosexuality and heterosexuality were evident in Ancient Greece, and they were seen as normal healthy beings. We are beginning to delve into many wider and broader terms of sexuality.

"Witchcraft does not need to apologize for involving sex magic. It is other religions which need to apologize for the miseries of puritanical repression they have inflicted on humanity"

Doreen Valiente (1922 – 1999)

English Author

Regular Sex and Masturbation is Key for Good Health

Everyone deserves to have a happy sex life. You don't have to look far on Google to find countless studies showing that sex is extremely beneficial to our health. This is because when we have sex, our brain fires up and activates various neurotransmitters, which serve our brain and several other organs.

Studies have shown that regular intimate sex and masturbation can: lower your blood pressure, helps strengthen your immune system, promotes better heart health, improve your self-esteem, improves your mood and mental well-being, reduces stress all over, increases your libido, offers pain relief and helps good sleep.

It does not matter what your lifestyle choice, situation, or preference is, and anyone can experience the benefits of sex.

It is thought that around eighty per cent of women do not have orgasms during penetrative sex. To achieve an orgasm, the mind and body must work together in a complex way. Unfortunately, there is so much shame around the human body that this stops people in their tracks. Body image has been scrutinised for many years, and the unobtainable perfect body image can cause a lot of anxiety. Whether conscious or not, women are more likely to block this pleasure experience in fear they are not perfect. It is about loving yourself unconditionally and seeing that you are perfect just the way you are. It is about *being* in the moment and being present in your body. Breathing deeply can help you relax and achieve orgasms. Balancing our bodies' masculine and feminine currents can help us express our sexuality free from negative and inhibiting feelings. Tantra and meditation can help achieve this.

Sex Power – Creating a Genius

Sex plays a significant part in our lives and our survival as a species. Napoleon Hill dedicates a whole chapter to sex in his "Think and Grow Rich" book. Napoleon Hill states

"The emotion of sex has behind it the possibility of three constructive potentialities:

1. The perpetuation of humankind.

2. The maintenance of health (as a therapeutic agency it has no equal).

3. The transformation of mediocrity into genius through transformation."

Napoleon Hill (1883-1970)
American Self-help Author

The emotion of sex brings you into another state of mind, which can transform energy into your desires. Sexual desires are strong and powerful emotions and bring about imagination and visualisation. When we channel this sex energy into something else, it takes willpower, but the rewards are great. I will discuss later this can be achieved through the Odic Force. You can ask any successful person, and they will tell you they have a healthy sex life. When someone has a highly developed sex nature, they have an irresistible magnetic force around them.

When the brain has been stimulated through sexual stimuli or something else, it changes the state of mind into a creative one. When in the creative state of mind, we become the Genius. The visionary state is a frame of mind where we receive *"hunches"*, *"sixth sense"*, or *"gut feelings"*. It is where our imagination and visualisation come to life. We operate on a higher frequency, and love and sex are high-frequency emotions. It is worth noting that sexual energy is not grounded but projected upwards to the mental/astral plains, which is why it is so powerful for manifestation. The channelled energy creates an astral image of the dominant thought at the moment of orgasm.

The Odic Force

A scientist called Baron von Reichenbach (1788 – 1869) discovered the *Odic Force*. The Odic Force is the underlying principle behind physical, electric and magnetic forces. Od can be seen as the fabric of the Universe, emanating from everything in various degrees. Liquid, crystals and metals retain the original Odic charge best, while silk is the only substance that will not absorb any additional Odic Energy. A scientist named Wilhelm Reich (1897 – 1957) inspired by this work discovered the *orgone*, a current that can be measured, also known as sexual and bioelectric energy. He published his findings in his book "*The Function of Orgasm*".

Odic Energy can be controlled and directed by the mind. This is the principle behind Magick. The Mind can create *thought forms* and imprint this onto an object by directing Odic Energy. Odic Energy can be channelled through deep breathing. First, the breath enters the lungs, which collect the energy. Next, the mind sends The Odic Energy thought forms created of mental imagery and emotional intensity through the blood. When the mind forms thought forms, it charges the blood with electromagnetically charged imagery. The blood imprints onto the Odic Energy accumulated in the lungs through deep breathing. Blood can also be charged through stimulation, such as orgasms or sexual stimuli. Releasing the charged breath onto the desired object or liquid then transfers the energy of your desire. The method of the Odic Breath is also known as *Informing*. Charging objects with the Odic Force can be a magnet for your wishes! Charging an object you carry with you daily, such as a piece of jewellery or a crystal, can keep your mind focused on what you are attracting to you.

Chapter Eight

Living in Magic

In this chapter, I will be looking at some tools that I used and that can help you live in Magic.

Giving and Receiving

"A hundred times a day I remind myself that my inner and outer life depend on the labors of other men, living and dead, and that I must exert myself in order to give in the same measure as I have received and am still receiving."

Albert Einstein (1879 – 1955)

Theoretical Physicist

Let's look at the act of giving. Do you give from a place of the heart, or are you measuring your good deeds? Do you give, so you have power and control over others? So you can hold them to your *"good"* deeds or *"favours"*? Or do you simply give from the heart? What we give, we receive. If we give from a place of greed or power, what we receive back will be limited.

Let's use a charity box as an example. You put ten pounds into a Charity box, and then you release with a shock that you put fifty pounds in, not ten pounds. You will only receive back the good for ten pounds. Why? Because you intended to put ten pounds in the box. It is all about the intention behind the money. So the fact you put fifty pounds in by accident doesn't matter. Lynne Twist has written a superb book that I highly recommend called *The Soul of Money*, and it changed everything for me.

Receiving and giving are all tied together. You've got to be open to receive, but you'll only ever be open to receive when you understand the concept of giving. This Universe has an order to it; remember the Universal Laws? What you see around you is part of your internal environment. You only receive from the Universe what you give to the Universe. That is why I always give away unwanted items of mine. I don't sell anything. I want them to go to a good home, where they can be used, or I give them to a charity so the funds from their sale can go to a good cause. I don't do this to receive, but the by-product is receiving from others. So what you have in your life is full of what you have received from what you have given for the greater good. If you want more good in your life, you must provide more of the greater good. You never have to worry about what you will receive because these fundamental laws govern the Universe. As you give, you receive. It is that simple. Now you don't have to give items, or money, but you can give time or kindness.

The Vacuum of Prosperity is such a beautiful concept because it follows nature. Nature hates vacuums. Let's take a sofa, for example, and you cannot put another sofa in place of the already present sofa until you get rid of the old one. It is why I tell people to release what is no longer serving them, as they cannot have new experiences or opportunities if they are holding onto old ones that do not serve a purpose. It is very much like the Death card in Tarot. Death means transformation. Your old life needs to end for your new one to begin; you cannot live two lives simultaneously. The old needs to be replaced with the new, as two things cannot simultaneously exist in the same space. You need to give the old away to receive the new. The fundamental Law behind giving is receiving. You need to give in abundance and willingness to receive graciously. It is all about intention and mindset. When you willingly give, that is an expression of a lot of faith based on understanding the Natural Laws.

"Your future is created by what you do today, not tomorrow."

Robert Kiyosaki (1947-)

American Entrepreneur, Businessman and Author

Giving Exercise

Start thinking about giving and receiving in your everyday life.

Who can you give to?

What can you give?

Where is this place of giving coming from?

Give to the best of your ability, and you will start receiving the best. It is all waiting for you. The Universe has an endless abundance.

Ask

You can continue to transform your life by starting to make small decisions that change the whole paradigm. One of the most powerful things you can start doing is asking for help when needed. We are taught not to *ask*. Our ego tells us not to *ask*. We feel small if we need help. I never used to ask for help; even when I fled domestic abuse and had nothing, I still didn't want to ask for help! But, when we take responsibility for our glorious future and step into the possibilities, we see the power of asking. When you study great men and women, look at how they sat at someone else feet and *asked*. Look at how their ego didn't get in the way of their service. When you don't want to ask for help, you let your ego get in the way, or you let fear get in the way. You experience the fear of how you will be perceived, the fear of disappointment, or the fear of rejection. Don't give your power away by thinking about other people's thoughts. It doesn't matter what other people think.

Knowing your limits and being able to ask for help is brilliance. Children ask questions to learn, and children ask when they need help. Children ask so they can thrive; children ask to build their social skills and develop relationships. So when did we stop asking? When did asking become uncomfortable?

Asking Exercise
In your journal, I want you to write about what areas of your life you need help and support. Then please ask for help from five people today.

The best version of you is on the other side of the knowledge you seek.

If you get a *no*, it means the *next opportunity*.

Journal this experience and write about what came up for you.

Don't get in your own way of achieving abundance, wealth and health!

The Need for a Tribe

"Wanting to identify with a tribe arguably is still a very important basic part of what it is to be human."

Chris Gibson

Professor of Human Geography

My first business Tribe was The Freedom Era, created by Jax Emilio Robinson. This has offered me more financial freedom than I could have imagined. It has taught me everything about authentic personal branding and leveraging social media to create a thriving online income. I have attracted so many like-minded souls into my life who have empowered me to create more freedom of choice and time. This platform became my Tribe, and from this Tribe, I have made my online business Tribe. Anyone who finds me on social media can request to join it. The wonderful thing is, you don't just have to be in one Tribe either! I have my Witches Coven that I set up and a Tribe of Soul Sisters who are not a part of the other Tribes. Remember, you are the average of the five people who surround you. Surround yourself with a loving, caring, and supportive tribe.

We all want to feel like we are part of something bigger. Without that feeling of belonging, we can fail to thrive. To feel like we belong is part of what it is to be human. A tribe, clan, coven, club, whatever you wish to call it, helps to provide a sense of purpose, a reason to engage with others, a form of expression, a form of support, a form of safety, and has many proven health and wellbeing benefits.

Finding a Tribe Exercise

A group of people coming together can be religious/faith-based and have a particular interest in art, history, charity, professional, cultural, academic, professional development, recreational or political.

Find your tribe if you don't already have one!

Think about what support it can offer you.

Is it right for you?

The Need for Movement

Movement is essential to good health and mental well-being. It is crucial for our energy levels and helps shift energy and release trauma or tension points in our bodies. We have been told for many years that exercise is the Miracle we have all been looking for. For good health, but it is more than that. It is self-love. It is making time for ourselves. It is carving that piece out of the day for *"just us"*. Our Health suffers when we do not exercise. It doesn't matter who you are, how healthy you eat, or how old or young you are; your health will suffer. Trauma is stored in the nervous system, so to "get it out", we need to move it out.

We know through strong scientific evidence that a physically active person is less likely to develop long-term (chronic) conditions such as depression, dementia, Alzheimer's disease, type 2 diabetes, cancer, and osteoarthritis, and are less like to fall and experience hip fractures.

So how much should we do? The National Health Service recommends the following:

- Under one year of age: 30 minutes of tummy time spread

throughout the day.

- One to two years of age: three hours of moderate activity spread throughout the day.

- Three to four years of age: two hours and one hour of moderate-to-vigorous intensity physical activity throughout the day.

- Five to eighteen years of age: This age group needs to do two types of exercise, aerobic and activities, to strengthen muscles and bones. Unfortunately, due to the school system, they are glued to a seat most of the day. This age should do as much as possible, but the recommended amount is one hour of moderate-to-vigorous intensity physical activity throughout the day.

- Nineteen to sixty-four: Three hours of moderate-intensity activity a week or 75 minutes of vigorous-intensity exercise a week. This also applies to people with additional needs, pregnant women and new Mothers!

- Sixty-five upwards: Three hours of moderate-intensity activity a week or 75 minutes of vigorous-intensity exercise a week.

Vigorous intensity means that your heart rate is beating fast and your breathing is heavy.

If you are already an active person, try and add an extra ten minutes to your routine. If inactive, start with ten minutes a day and build this up. Choose whatever works for you. It could be a short brisk walk on a lunch break or dancing to music while cleaning the house. Find a form of movement you enjoy and take it from there. If you struggle with motivation, you are not alone. Your brain is programmed to avoid pain, seek pleasure and conserve energy. Invite a friend to motivate you and do it together, or download an app so you can be prompted and you can see your progress. I remember I used to struggle with my exercises. I could never find time, or my child was always trying to jump me. So I bought a bike and got a second-hand children's bike seat off Facebook Marketplace. For the nights he went to sleep on time, I followed an exercise DVD while watching a film on the TV. I had my laptop playing the DVD under the TV and created my new habit this way.

This section is not about having optiMum health but about *feeling* better, the *feeling* of having more energy, the *feeling* of self-love, and the *feeling* of having healthy habits.

Natalie Fawkes

Personal Trainer

When our brains are in a negative mindset, everything around us, no matter how positive, will always draw the negatives out. This is because our brains are the centre of our worlds; we are controlled by our brains. Some things we control with our thoughts, and for others, our brains take the lead. Either

---

way, our brain is an amazing and very clever tool that we do not use to its full potential.

When people think about exercise, many will see it as a negative; 'it makes me hot and sweaty, 'it makes me tired, 'I use energy I don't have, 'I'm tired or 'I don't have the time. These are just a few common thoughts about exercise, but actually, by exercising, we are also giving our brains a workout without even realising it. Exercising is not just good for your health but also for your mental health. Having a focus when it's just you and your thoughts whilst you exercise is a positive connection we all need. It's a time to connect, breathe, and process thoughts or feelings without realising you're doing such a thing. There are various types of exercise we can do, but we need to explore the options. We see it as 'exercising at the gym', but there are sports and clubs, swimming and hiking, for example. Whatever you enjoy, you can turn that exercise into a positive.

I found exercise after coming out of a long-term unhealthy toxic relationship. One that I was in denial about for many years and would fight the hurt almost every day. Soon after, I realised my hate for myself, the feeling uncomfortable in my skin and how I looked, and I needed to change. I had been emotionally beaten down so much during my relationship that I couldn't see who I was or who I should and wanted to be. I was just a brain, in a body, on autopilot.

I decided I needed a new focus and reason to love myself

again and discover who I was as a person again. The person that was still deep inside. I'd always enjoyed sports and exercise growing up, so I knew turning to exercise a way to help my mind and have a new focus. I found the more I moved and tried new workouts and forms of exercise, the happier I started to feel. A smile returned, and I began to like the person I saw staring back at me in the mirror. Finding this new focus had such a positive impact on me; I wanted to help others, encouraging people around me how they could experience a positive change too. The enjoyment I got from helping others encouraged me to train to be a Personal trainer. It was a way to help others and the way exercise had helped me. It allows me to help change their health for the better and their mental health without them realising it.

Be brave; push those barriers aside and your opinions about exercise. Instead, try different exercises and sports to see what you enjoy. Then, see how you feel after completing your workout, and note how to feel the following day. I promise you, and you'll feel great.

Good luck x

Prayer for Healing

When we pray for healing or for another to receive healing, we trust that the Divine will offer that healing. We know we won't be given the power to do it ourselves, but we know the Divine/Infinite Mind will do the healing. There is a saying that a Doctor can put a plaster on the wound, but *God* does the healing. When we pray, the conscious mind makes a powerful suggestion of health to the subconscious mind, and healing takes place. When we send healing to another, we send a powerful suggestion of health through the Divine to the other person's subconscious mind, and their subconscious mind heals the body. Remember, we are all connected.

So what forms of Healing are there, and how does it work?

Natural, Spiritual, Hands-on Healing or Distant Healing is an ancient therapy which involves the transference of energy from one person to another. The person with the intent to heal (through prayer) channels energy from the Universe, and it flows into the recipient's whole being, healing their physical body and also emotionally, mentally and spiritually. Channelling this energy, and with intent, assists your own energy systems in bringing about the healing you need.

There is no religious belief that is at variance with spiritual healing. It is an ancient art that has been practised across all cultures worldwide.

Jackie Barber

Pure Balance Therapy

https://purebalancetherapy.co.uk/

What is Healing?

As a nutrition and food intolerance consultant, I never had a deliberate plan to move into Healing. However, I began to become aware that something was missing from some of my clients. There needed to be more than good food and supplementation to give them the desired results.

I met a therapist almost by chance who told me about Rahanni Celestial Healing. When I researched Rahanni further, I just knew that I just had to learn it! This was the beginning of my journey into Healing. Later I studied (and still teach) Spiritual/Natural Healing with The Healing Foundation to give me a much wider understanding of the subject.

If I had to describe Healing, I would say that it brings you back to the true essence of You. It gives calm, peace and balance, but it also energises, boosts, and restores the physical body, mind, and soul. There are many ways that Healing can help you. It can reduce stress, anxiety, depression, and physical pain. Because it increases immunity, energy, confidence, and awareness – personal development is an obvious benefit too!

A Healer will gently place their hands on you (or in your aura) and channel pure energy through themselves to then pass to you, the recipient. You will feel yourself begin to settle as the Healing flows through you. It is a beautiful sensation; the best way to understand it is to experience it. Even today, I still think of Healing as a little bit of magic that I am very fortunate to be able to share with people of all ages from all walks of life. I like that the Healing I channel and teach has no set religion. Instead, it comes from a place of pure love and compassion.

The Healer will always set an intention at the beginning of the session. The intention is that the recipient should receive healing for their 'highest good. This means that the healer does not choose the outcome; they trust that what is most needed for the individual at that time is what they receive. Overall, the recipient will enjoy calm and relaxation; when this happens, the Healing journey will begin….

Now, as Principal of The Healing Foundation, I get to support Healers from around the UK personally. Our training meets the National Occupational Standard for Healing, and by maintaining the highest standards of professionalism, we can protect both the public and our accredited Members.

Healing, for me, is an honour, a privilege, and a highly rewarding vocation.

Tarot

There is such a fine line between Tarot Readings and Counselling. Tarot Readings come with a great responsibility as the Reader needs to be able to hold the client in a sacred and sensitive space. There are many types of Readings, such as Divination, Enlightenment, Spirit Communication, Guidance, Empowerment, and Past Life. The Reader uses storytelling, intuition and visualisation to receive messages and make sense of the spread in front of them. Different Tarot Decks have different amounts of cards and styles. Still, traditionally, seventy-eight cards are divided into two groups: the major arcana, which has twenty-two cards, and the minor arcana, which has fifty-six cards. The Reader puts themselves in the heart of the reading where guidance is sought. Here is a place where questions can be asked, and answers received.

I have had to navigate my way through some challenging situations. I had support from family and friends, but even their knowledge had limits, and no one had been in my situation before. It was new to everyone involved, and sometimes it was overwhelming, emotionally charged, and logic felt like a distant memory at times. Some days I felt like there was no way out, and I had no idea what direction to go. I felt stuck, anxious, fearful, lonely, and lost.

The Tarot Cards were my lifeline. They gave a different perspective; they never judge, don't argue, don't put you down, don't get frustrated or angry, and never doubt you. Instead, they empowered me and helped me to see the light at the end of the tunnel.

Now I can use my gift to help others, which is incredibly rewarding.

Now let us ask a serious question that I get asked all the time.

Is there such a thing as a bad Tarot Reading?

No, absolutely not! There are no such things as bad Tarot Readings or bad cards. If you are ever told this you are not seeking a reading from a professional, I would not go ahead with them. I have heard many horror stories where people are told when they will die and other things. I was horrified! Even if such a message were to come through, a professional would never disclose this information, as nothing is written in stone. I become genuinely upset when I hear of people's bad or negative experiences with Tarot Readers.

Tarot Readings are about invoking and gaining hindsight, insight and foresight. Remember, *your* future is in *your own* hands. So rather than predicting the future, the cards test out multiple scenarios and find the best solution.

Crystal Magic

Gemstones attract people all over the world, and they are

prized possessions. Diamonds, Emeralds, Rubies, and Sapphires are precious stones, but semi-precious stones are equally just as cherished and have been for thousands of years. Gemstones are not only ornaments or jewellery, but each has a sacred meaning and healing power. Gemstones are also used in many of our advanced machines today; for example, Garnet and Rubies are used in Laser technology. Certain types of crystals are known to absorb and emit energies. Sodalite, Tourmaline and Rose Quartz can be placed next to computers and other devices to reduce radiation. I work with a large chunk of Rose Quartz on my desk to absorb anything from my laptop.

Crystals have an extremely high vibration that can raise levels of your consciousness and have the ability to open the higher Chakras. The Crystal Kingdom is vast, and there are many resources readily available if this is something you feel drawn to. I personally use the three-book Crystal Bible Volumes by Judy Hall.

Abby Elizabeth Smith

Celestial Coven

https://www.celestialcoven.co.uk/

Since as early as c.4500, civilizations have used Crystals and their associated powers for healing and magic formulas. Whilst the world has changed and evolved, Crystals have remained a constant in society for some individuals. Mysticism has, like all trends, had its moments of being taboo and being all the rage. As a Crystal Lover, I'm lucky to be in an age where Crystals, Witchcraft and other Spiritual Healing practices are gaining respect and are celebrated, plus gaining popularity by the year!

Although Crystals are popular, common and necessary practices are less well known. As the owner of a Crystal Business, as well as providing affordable and authentic Crystals, I also offer educational information, whether that be through my blog or Social Media posts, to provide awareness and education within the community. So, when the opportunity arose to write a section in this book, I wanted to share some of the common questions I have been asked so that you can feel more educated when buying and using Crystals!

Can I buy Crystals just for decoration?

Absolutely! If you are drawn to Crystals because of their healing properties and energy, wonderful! If you're drawn to Crystals because they look pretty and you would like them in your space or wear, they are also wonderful! If you want to own Crystals, own them.

What does Cleansing or Charging mean?

Cleansing means cleansing the energy from the Crystal; this could be removing negative energy that it has absorbed from your surroundings.

"Charging" means charging the energy within the Crystal, which is why it is important to cleanse the Crystal before charging, as you certainly don't want to charge negative energy!

How do I know what healing properties Crystals have?

Research! Like anything, research is the key. However, ensure you use reliable sources to carry out your research. Here are my top Crystals for a beginner who is undertaking crystal healing!

Green Aventurine, for Luck and Prosperity – Golden Healer, for aligning your Chakras – Lepidolite, for Anxiety relief – Pyrite, for balancing your emotions – Selenite, for Cleansing – Amethyst, for Stress relief – Sodalite, for enhancing your communication – Clear Quartz, for amplifying the healing effects of the other Crystals – Peach Moonstone, for calming your mind – Obsidian, for Protection against negative energy – Rose Quartz, for Self-Love – Citrine, for cleansing your Aura, and increasing optimism – Lapis Lazuli, for Wisdom and intuition – Tigers Eye, for Confidence.

The questions regarding Crystals and Crystal Healing are endless, but with some patience and an open mind, you can find your answers. Then, you can carry out all the research you need and learn everything about them, and use these four billion-year-old rocks to enhance your vibes, energy and life!

"What the mind of man can conceive and believe, the mind of man can achieve."

Napoleon Hill (1883-1970)

American Self-help Author

Thank you for reading this book, and thank you for embarking on a journey of self-love. We are all connected, so my lovely reader, when I say I love you, I do.

"If we are related, we have, through these pages, met."

Napoleon Hill (1883-1970)

American Self-help Author

So mote it be

Kitty

Reference

"Come Lord Jesus,

Be our guest,

And let these gifts

To us be blest.

Amen." — Anonymous Schmitz, J. (2021) *Tisch-Gebetgen - German orgins, Bedtime.* Available at: https://www.bedtime.com/tisch-gebetgen-german-orgins/

"A thankful person is thankful under all circumstances. A complaining soul complains even in paradise." — Bahá'u'lláh (*A quote by bahá'u'lláh* (no date) *Goodreads.* Goodreads. Available at: https://www.goodreads.com/quotes/631935-a-thankful-person-is-thankful-under-all-circumstances-a-complaining)

"It has been proven now scientifically that an affirmative thought is hundreds of times more powerful than a negative thought." — Bernard, Michael. Beckwith, (no date) "A Complete Guide to Using the Law of Attraction," *Jack Canfield Maximizing Your Potential.* Self Esteem Seminars. Available at: https://jackcanfield.com/blog/using-the-law-of-attraction/.

"All that we are is the result of what we have thought." — *Buddha,* (no date) "A Complete Guide to Using the Law of

Attraction," *Jack Canfield Maximizing Your Potential*. Self Esteem Seminars. Available at: https://jackcanfield.com/blog/using-the-law-of-attraction/.

"The Law of Attraction allows for infinite possibilities, infinite abundance, and infinite joy. It knows no order of difficulty, and it can change your life in every way if you let it." —Canfield, Jack. (no date) "A Complete Guide to Using the Law of Attraction," Jack Canfield Maximizing Your Potential. Self Esteem Seminars. Available at: https://jackcanfield.com/blog/using-the-law-of-attraction/.

"We can hardly bear to look. The shadow may carry the best of the live we have not lived. Go into the basement, the attic, the refuse bin. Find gold there. Find an animal who has not been fed or watered. It is you!! This neglected, exiled animal, hungry for attention, is a part of yourself." — Cope, Stephen. (2012) Great work of your life. Random House Usa Inc.

"And above all, watch with glittering eyes the whole world around you because the greatest secrets are always hidden in the most unlikely places. Those who don't believe in magic will never find it." — Dahl, Roald. and Benson, P. (2009) The Minpins. New York: Puffin Books.

"No Man Is an Island." — Donne, John, Lush, H. (1988) No man is an Island. London: Souvenir.

"I admit thoughts influence the body." — Einstein, *Albert.* (no date) "A Complete Guide to Using the Law of Attraction," *Jack*

Canfield *Maximizing Your Potential*. Self Esteem Seminars. Available at: https://jackcanfield.com/blog/using-the-law-of-attraction/.

"A hundred times a day I remind myself that my inner and outer life depend on the labors of other men, living and dead, and that I must exert myself in order to give in the same measure as I have received and am still receiving." — Einstein, *Albert.* (Byrne, R. (2012) *The magic.* London etc.: Simon & Schuster.)

"The conscious mind may be compared to a fountain playing in the sun and falling back into the great subterranean pool of subconscious from which it rises." — Freud, Sigmund. Ananthaswamy, A. (2016) *neurologic: The enthralling story of the unconscious mind, New Scientist.* New Scientist. Available at: https://www.newscientist.com/article/2076606-neurologic-the-enthralling-story-of-the-unconscious-mind/

"Visualisation is the great secret of success." — Gallagher, Sandy. *Visualisation is the great secret of success* (2020) *YouTube.* YouTube. Available at: https://www.youtube.com/watch?v=SGnNm_oZTXE

"Wanting to identify with a tribe arguably is still a very important basic part of what it is to be human." — Gibson, Chris. (no date) *The importance of finding your tribe—university of wollongong, University of Wollongong.* The Stand. Available at: https://www.uow.edu.au/the-stand/2017/the-importance-of-finding-your-tribe.php.

"The emotion os sex has behind it the possibility of three constructive potentialities:

1. The perpetuation of humankind.

2. The maintenance of health (as a therapeutic agency it has no equal).

3. The transformation of mediocrity into genius through transformation." — Hill, Napoleon. (2004) *Think and grow rich: Napoleon hill., revised and expanded by dr. Arthur R. Pell*. London: Vermilion.

"What the mind of man can conceive and believe, the mind of man can achieve." — Hill, Napoleon. (2004) *Think and grow rich: Napoleon hill., revised and expanded by dr. Arthur R. Pell*. London: Vermilion.

"If we are related, we have, through these pages, met." — Hill, Napoleon. (2004) *Think and grow rich: Napoleon hill., revised and expanded by dr. Arthur R. Pell*. London: Vermilion.

"Knowledge is a treasure, but practice is the key to it." — Iban Khaldoun Al Muqaddima. (1332-1406). Byrne, R. (2012) *The magic*. London etc.: Simon & Schuster.

"Your future is created by what you do today, not tomorrow." — Kiyosaki, Robert. (no date) "A Complete Guide to Using the Law of Attraction," *Jack Canfield Maximizing Your Potential*. Self Esteem Seminars. Available at: https://jackcanfield.com/blog/using-the-law-of-attraction/.

The Law of Mentalism

"The All is Mind

- *the Universe is Mental"* — The Kybalion. Initiates, T. (2018) *Kybalion: Centenary edition.* Penguin Publishing Group.

The Law of Vibration

"Nothing rests;

everything moves;

everything vibrates" — The Kybalion. Initiates, T. (2018) *Kybalion: Centenary edition.* Penguin Publishing Group.

The Law of Rhythm

"Everything flows, out and in;

everything has its tides;

all things rise and fall;

the pendulum-swing manifests in everything:

the measure of the swing to the right is the measure of the swing to the left;

rhythm compensates" — The Kybalion. Initiates, T. (2018) *Kybalion: Centenary edition.* Penguin Publishing Group.

The Law of Polarity

"Everything is Dual;

everything has poles;

everything has its pair of opposites;

like and unlike are the same;

opposites are identical in Nature, but different in degree;

extremes meet;

all truths are but half-truths;

all paradoxes can be reconciled" — The Kybalion. Initiates, T. (2018) *Kybalion: Centenary edition*. Penguin Publishing Group.

The Law of Cause and Effect

"Every Cause has its Effect;

- *every Effect has its Cause;*

- *everything happens according to Law;*

- *Chance is but a name for Law not recognised;*

- *there are many planes of causation, but nothing escapes the Law"* — The Kybalion. Initiates, T. (2018) *Kybalion: Centenary edition*. Penguin Publishing Group.

The Law of Gender

"Gender is in everything;

• *everything has its Masculine and Feminine Principles;*

• *gender manifests on all planes."* — The Kybalion. Initiates, T. (2018) *Kybalion: Centenary edition*. Penguin Publishing Group.

"As above, so below, as within, so without, as the Universe, so the soul." —Trismegistus, Hermes. The Kybalion. Initiates, T. (2018) *Kybalion: Centenary edition*. Penguin Publishing Group.

"All men dream; but not equally. Those who dream by night in the dusty recesses of their minds Awake to find that it was vanity; But the dreamers of day are dangerous men. That they may act their dreams with open eyes to make it possible." — Lawrence, T.E.. projects, C.to W. (2022) T. E. Lawrence, Wikiquote. Wikimedia Foundation, Inc. Available at: https://en.wikiquote.org/wiki/T._E._Lawrence

"To believe in the things you can see and touch is no belief at all; but to believe in the unseen is a triumph and a blessing." — Lincoln, Abraham. Proctor, Bob. (2002) *You were born rich: Now you can discover and develop those riches*. Scottsdale, AZ: LifeSuccess Productions.

"If thou canst believe, all things are possible to him that believeth." — "MARK 9:23 (2017) in *The Holy Bible: Combining the old and new testaments translated out of the original tongues and with the former translations diligently compared and revised: Authorized king James Version*. Nashville, TN: Thomas Nelson.

"What things soever ye desire, when ye pray,

believe that ye receive them,

and ye shall have them." — MARK 11:24 (2017) in *The Holy Bible: Combining the old and new testaments translated out of the original tongues and with the former translations diligently compared and revised: Authorized king James Version.* Nashville, TN: Thomas Nelson.

"The brightest flame casts the darkest shadow." — Martin, George R.R. (2011), in A clash of kings: Book two of a song of ice and fire. London: Harper Voyager.

"Let Go And Let God." — Proctor, Bob. (2002) *You were born rich: Now you can discover and develop those riches.* Scottsdale, AZ: LifeSuccess Productions.

"Success is the progressive realization of a worthy ideal." — Nightingale, Earl. Zierman, B. (2018) *Success is the progressive realization of a worthy ideal, Boundary Dispute Law Blog.* Justice Smiles. Available at: https://www.boundarydisputelaw.com/enjoy/success-is-the-progressive-realization-of-a-worthy-ideal#:~:text=Earl%20Nightingale%20who%20was%20mentored,Realization%20of%20a%20Worthy%20Ideal.%E2%80%9D

"Most people tiptoe their way through life, hoping they make it safely to death." — Nightingale, Earl. Thakur, A. (2021) Earl Nightingale quote: Most people tiptoe their way through life,

hoping they make it safely to death., Minimalist Quotes. Available at: https://minimalistquotes.com/earl-nightingale-quote-97421/

"Trying harder" isn't necessarily the solution to achieving more. It may not offer any real promise for getting what you want out of life. Sometimes, in fact, it's a big part of the problem.

If you stake your hopes for a breakthrough on trying harder than ever, you may kill your chances for success." — Pritchett, Price. (2012) "A True Story," in *You²: A high velocity formula for multiplying your personal effectiveness in quantum leaps.* Dallas, TX: Pritchett.

"To let life happen to you is irresponsible. To create your day is your divine right." — Ramtha. (no date) "A Complete Guide to Using the Law of Attraction," *Jack Canfield Maximizing Your Potential.* Self Esteem Seminars. Available at: https://jackcanfield.com/blog/using-the-law-of-attraction/.

"Trauma bonding is the attachment an abused person feels for their abuser, specifically in a relationship with a cyclical pattern of abuse. The bond is created due to a cycle of abuse and positive reinforcement." — Resnick, Ariane. C.N.C. (2021) What is trauma bonding?, Verywell Mind. Verywell Mind. Available at: https://www.verywellmind.com/trauma-bonding-5207136

"If you do what you've always done, you'll get what you've

always gotten." — Robbins, Anthony. (no date) "A Complete Guide to Using the Law of Attraction," *Jack Canfield Maximizing Your Potential*. Self Esteem Seminars. Available at: https://jackcanfield.com/blog/using-the-law-of-attraction/.

"We are only ever mirrors of each other." — Robinson, Jax. (2022) *Jax Emilio Robinson, Facebook*. Available at: https://www.facebook.com/jackstar.lou.

"I hear many speak about changing a paradigm in concept but without the substance of realising that we can only change our own paradigm to impact the entire paradigm. And changing it simply means to choose LOVE in situations that we as a society justify to LOVE LESS..." — Robinson, Jax. (2022) *Jax Emilio Robinson, Facebook*. Available at: https://www.facebook.com/jackstar.lou.

"People are just as wonderful as sunsets if I can let them be. When I look at a sunset, I don't find myself saying, "Soften the orange a little on the right-hand corner, and put a bit more purple along the base, and use a little more pink in the cloud colour." I don't do that. I don't try to control a sunset. I watch it with awe as it unfolds." — Rogers, Carl., 1980. *A Way of Being*, Houghton Mifflin, 1980: 22.

"You're the average of the five people spend the most time with." — Rohn, Jim. (2020) *You're the average of the five people spend the most time with.*, Quotelia. Available at: https://quotelia.com/youre-the-average-of-the-five-people

"We are a way for the Universe to know itself. Some part of our being knows this is where we came from. We long to return. And we can, because the cosmos is also within us. We're made of star stuff." — Sagan, Carl. Author Victor de la Cruz (2018) *"we're made of Star Stuff. we are a way for the cosmos to know itself.", My Geek Wisdom.* Available at: https://mygeekwisdom.com/2018/02/17/were-made-of-star-stuff-we-are-a-way-for-the-cosmos-to-know-itself/

"Tough times never last, but tough people do." — Schuller, Robert.H. (1988) *Tough times never last, but tough people do!* New Delhi: Orient Paperbacks.

"The first step is you have to say that you can." — Smith, Will. Will smith quotes (no date) BrainyQuote. Xplore. Available at: https://www.brainyquote.com/quotes/will_smith_451158

"I love to win.

I love to grind, hustle and get it done.

I don't love feeling my whole body ache, getting sick, or scrolling mindlessly on social media to escape the suppressed feelings I avoided while I was in the DOING, DOING, DOING of it all.

But many find themselves stuck in a looping experience of Doing vs Being.

So...it isn't about learning to "let go" of Doing, or to even do less.

It's about CHANNELING our DOING.

Into more of what we love.

So the thrill of being in the masculine, becomes a Way of Being.

And allows the Inner Masculine to lead us to victory, without it being a hostile takeover!

... to dissolve the pattern and looping process of burnout and energetic overflow.

And replace it with integration, flow and total freedom in who you BE." — Tan, Berenice (2022) *Berenice Tan (Breathwork Teacher Trainer), Facebook.* Berenice Tan. Available at: https://www.facebook.com/ber.tan.9

"Witchcraft does not need to apologize for involving sex magic. It is other religions which need to apologize for the miseries of puritanical repression they have inflicted on humanity." — Valiente, Doreen. (2005) *Witchcraft for Tomorrow.* London: Robert Hale.

"You live inside this omnipresent mind of all... the entire Universe (including yourself and your life) is composed of an all-encompassing Divine mind, its thoughts, and thought form.... Your true mind (your Higher Self) is an extension and a creation of the Divine Mind."— Virtue, Doreen. (2006) Divine *magic: The seven sacred secrets of manifestation.* Carlsbad, CA: Hay House.

"To live is the rarest thing in the world. Most people exist, that is all." — Wilde, Oscar. Goodreads. Available at: https://www.goodreads.com/quotes/2448-to-live-is-the-rarest-thing-in-the-world-most

"Third Law of motion…every action has an equal and opposite reaction…It doesn't matter what you do unto others, it's already been done to you." — Winfrey, Oprah. Smith, J. (2015) *Oprah Winfrey speaks on a meaningful life at Harry's Last lecture, The Stanford Daily.* Available at: https://stanforddaily.com/2015/04/21/oprah-winfrey-speaks-on-a-meaningful-life-at-harrys-last-lecture/

About the Author

"I know where I am going because I know where I have been."

Kitty started her journey of self-discovery when she studied to become a fully qualified THF Healer. From there, she discovered her gifts as a Psychic Medium and now identifies as a Witch. These gifts helped her navigate challenging situations, including fleeing domestic abuse and coercive control. Kitty suffered years of emotional, psychological, and financial abuse. As a result, she lacked confidence and self-esteem, and her physical health seriously suffered. This all changed when she discovered her unconditioned inner Magic. Unfortunately, she is also a missed ectopic pregnancy survivor and was in and out of the hospital sixteen times over three months due to complications. This was a traumatic and heart-wrenching experience for her. Due to a high tolerance for anaesthetics, Kitty also experienced the trauma of being awake during her heart procedure, where she could speak and move and was in immense pain.

Kitty trained herself to use Tarot Cards and later studied counselling to merge with her childcare qualification, where she studied child development. Using holistic practices and traditional counselling, Kitty started her journey of healing from trauma. Combining the two, she then studied The Natural Universal Laws and experienced life-changing results.

Kitty has now set up multiple income streams as a Psychic Medium, Quantum Leap Facilitator, Author, creator of Pagan Roots MoonTea and Entrepreneur. She is also honoured to be part of The Freedom Era Platform, *"a global community of conscious entrepreneurs who are committed to bringing forth a paradigm shift in how we do business and life."* They have become her tribe, community and family. Kitty also advocates for domestic abuse and coercive control survivors and is a proud single mum to her beautiful son, Harrison.

Kitty helps entrepreneurs build profitable businesses from the core of who they are and teaches them how to use their intuition and change their paradigms to reshape their world.

Kitty helps individuals navigate their way through life and find their soul calling. The methods she uses include Spiritual Readings, Tarot Readings and Spiritual Healing. These safe and gentle methods can help you understand your patterns and behaviours to overcome negative blocks and enjoy greater happiness, health and love.

They can also offer words of empowerment, clarity, and guidance.

Printed in Great Britain
by Amazon

20221699R00129